THE LATIN AMERICAN CITY

Alan Gilbert

THE LATIN AMERICAN CITY

Alan Gilbert

The Latin America Bureau is an independent research and publishing organisation. It works to broaden public understanding of human rights and social and economic justice in Latin America and the Caribbean.

First published in the UK in 1994 by the Latin America Bureau
(Research and Action) Ltd, 1 Amwell Street, London EC1R 1UL

A CIP catalogue record for the book is available from the British Library

ISBN 0 906156 82 3 (pbk)
ISBN 0 906156 83 1 (hbk)

Editor: James Ferguson

Cover photograph: Bruno Barbey/Magnum
Cover design: Andy Dark

Printed and bound by Russell Press, Nottingham NG7 3HN
Trade distribution in UK by Central Books, 99 Wallis Road, London E9 5LN
Distribution in North America by Monthly Review Press, 122 West 27th Street,
New York, NY 10001

CONTENTS

Tables

Figures

1

THE URBAN LANDSCAPE

In many ways, Latin American cities look very similar. They are all highly unequal and contain wide extremes of poverty and affluence. Urban sprawl has produced almost identical suburbs, so that it is difficult to tell either the shanty towns or the high-income residential areas in one city from those in another. The ubiquitous bootblack, street vendor and beggar frequent the central streets of every major city along with elegantly dressed business people and government workers. Traffic congestion, skyscrapers and street children are found everywhere.

At the same time, every Latin American city is different. The look and feel of Tijuana, Oaxaca, Salvador, Buenos Aires and Lima reflect major differences in culture, climate, poverty and economic function. While I feel that there are enough bonds linking this range of places together to justify writing a book entitled the Latin American City, I want to begin by emphasising their diversity.

The following descriptions of five Latin American cities show the differences that exist across the region. The descriptions include cities from Mexico in the north through Spanish South America to Portuguese-speaking Brazil. La Paz, with its poor, indigenous population living up in the clouds is the archetypal Andean city. Rio de Janeiro with its cultural kaleidoscope, its beaches and sunshine, its life and glamour is in a very different world. Bogotá is different again; a poor city but, unlike most in Latin America, one that became no poorer during the 1980s. Caracas, with its motorways and skyscrapers, looks very much like a North American city; only its hillsides full of shanty towns remind visitors that it most certainly is not. Finally, Guadalajara, seemingly a pearl of Mexican tidiness and civility, stands in apparent contradiction to the patent disorder so obvious in the other cities. Is the real Latin America shown best by the social tranquillity of Guadalajara or in the bubbling unpredictability of Rio de Janeiro? Is the economic resilience of Bogotá the norm, or the dire poverty of La Paz?

Santafé de Bogotá

Flying into Bogotá means crossing the Andes. Below, the green, undulating slopes of the eastern *cordillera* are covered by the small coffee farms that for so long sustained the Colombian economy. Then, about forty miles from the airport, the landscape changes; a flat plateau spreads out surrounded by a ring of mountains. Coffee cultivation gives way to dairy farming and to fields of maize, potatoes and vegetables. Plastic greenhouses are everywhere, accommodating Colombia's newest boom product, fresh-cut flowers. In a few miles, the climate has changed from semi-tropical to temperate.

Bogotá huddles against the eastern rim of mountains, with the *sabana* stretching out in three directions. On top of the mountains, two thousand feet above the centre of the city are two great religious symbols, the convent of Monserrate and the giant statue of Guadalupe. These monuments to piety once dominated the whole city. Today, they can still be seen from most parts of Bogotá, even if their religious significance has undoubtedly declined. Unlike Caracas or Rio de Janeiro, Bogotá has few physical constraints on its expansion.

Located at 8,600 feet, Bogotá's climate is cool and it rains frequently. Colombians from other parts of the country say that the climate matches the *cachaco* persona: cool and reserved. The city is grey, lacking the warmth of the coastal areas, the vibrancy of the coffee regions, the colour of the Cauca valley. These comments reveal the stereotypes that are embedded in Colombian regional sentiment. The images are real but misleading in an important respect: Bogotá is no longer a regional centre. Today, it is the most Colombian of cities for the simple reason that it is full of migrants from other parts of the country.

Like most large Latin American cities, Bogotá has grown rapidly. In 1938 it had 350,000 people, by 1964 it had 1.7 million, today it has 5.2 million. In little more than fifty years its population has grown around fifteen fold. Migration from the countryside began in a big way in the 1930s, magnified by the rural violence that has been such a recurrent theme in Colombian political life. People came from every part of the country, although the bulk of the new arrivals came from the two nearby departments of Cundinamarca and Boyacá. Today, fewer than half of the inhabitants were born outside the city, the consequence of earlier migrants bearing their children in the alien urban environment. Migrants continue to arrive in the city, but the pace of urban growth has slowed down. Between 1973 and 1985 Bogotá's population grew annually by only three per cent.

From a distance, Bogotá looks anything but the supposedly impoverished Latin American metropolis. The skyscrapers and office blocks

Bogotá: the mountain backcloth dwarfs the central skyscrapers   author's photo

of the central city are dwarfed by the backcloth of mountains. From the airport the visitor travelling to the centre of town passes modern factories and the local offices of world-famous companies. Overpasses take traffic across the four-lane motorway. If many of the cars are less than smart, the Mazdas and Renaults which dominate the traffic are recognisably modern vehicles. On arrival at the Tequendama hotel, it is likely that the traveller has seen little in the way of poverty.

Looking out from the hotel window in the morning, there are few signs of shanties. Most of the buildings are solidly constructed and only later does one notice the distant flanks of the mountains with their higgledy-piggledy housing, clearly too small and untidy to be middle-class. But self-help housing in Bogotá, even though it houses most of the people, is not flimsy. At night the climate is sufficiently cold to guarantee that most homes have solid walls. When I first went to the city it took me a week to find a 'proper' shanty town.

But few visitors go to the low-income areas of the city. They mainly stay in the central area and travel to the sanitised northern suburbs. Around the Country Club and the Unicentro shopping mall, the large areas of expensive housing give off a reassuring feel of affluence. Of course, there are some poor people on the streets, pulling hand carts containing recycled refuse, cleaning shoes and selling newspapers; they can be seen looking out of the overcrowded buses passing through. But they impinge little on the scene. The north of Bogotá is typical of the way that Latin American elites have managed to create areas of 'modernity' amidst vast surrounding expanses of poverty.

Should the visitor move further north or travel to the segregated south of the city, a different world appears. The shops are smaller and offer a more limited range of goods. The streets in the commercial centres contain different kinds of people. They speak the same language and they are dressed in 'proper' clothes, but they are darker, smaller, and obviously much poorer. Take the bus to the end of the route, and the urban environment deteriorates. The road acquires increasing numbers of pot-holes and eventually runs out of tarmac. The housing gradually becomes more rudimentary, revealing the self-help nature of the building process. The plots are laid out in a regular pattern, but every house looks very different. Each family has built what it can afford. One plot has a well-constructed two-storey home, the next a rickety shack. These low-income areas are not invasion settlements or squatter communities, for the poor have bought their plots of land. Initially, the settlements lacked all services and some communities had to petition for years before they obtained electricity, water, drainage and schools.

These people are different from others in Bogotá only in the sense that they are much poorer. They are 'marginal' to Bogotá society only in the sense that they live on the edge of the city. Most can read and write and most children go to school. Few are politically active, and many are ardent Catholics who spend some of their weekend helping to build a new church. Many work in the 'formal' economy as factory workers, builders, shop-workers and government employees. Even those employed in the 'informal sector' are scarcely marginal; the vendors are selling manufactured products, cigarettes, ice cream, chewing gum and newspapers. There are few beggars in this part of the city and, unlike the central areas, there are few street-sellers. Most of the local commerce operates from small shops and from improvised counters in people's front rooms.

What is it like to live in one of these settlements? In terms of the quality of shelter, it all depends. Some of the houses are spacious and well-constructed, others are extremely flimsy. Some settlements are well-serviced, but most new neighbourhoods will suffer from years of neglect. Between 1974 and 1980 Britalia, in the southwest of the city, had few taps, no drainage and no paved streets. When it rained the streets were almost impassable with thick mud. Many parts of the settlement suffered from a foul smell because pools of sewage filled the drainage ditches. Today, the settlement is linked to the drainage system and nearly all of the roads are paved. In a few years the settlement was transformed.

Bogotá: the settlement of Britalia eighteen years after foundation   author's photo

The transformation, however, was not without cost. The community had to demand water and drainage. The Water Company was reluctant to service the settlement because the community did not have title deeds, because the authorities were investigating the activities of the developer, and principally because the settlement lay below the level of the River Bogotá. If water were to be installed, then drainage would be needed. But to provide drains that worked would require a pump to move the water into the river. A satisfactory electric pump would be expensive and the Company wanted to be sure that the population was prepared to pay for its installation and maintenance. The community sent delegations on many occasions to the Water Company. In the end, a deal was struck: the community would pay a deposit of 30 per cent of the cost of the installation and pay off the rest over a four-year period. The community organisation started collecting the money.

Getting to work from low-income settlements is always a problem. Casablanca, in the Suba district of Bogotá, was off the bus route for ten years. Workers had to walk ten minutes to the nearest bus route and then hope that the buses would not be too full to pick them up. Now buses reach the settlement, even if they fail to provide an adequate service. Although few Bogotá drivers are averse to speeding, the buses move slowly because of the dense traffic and because of the frequent stops they make whenever

Bogotá: Búlevar Niza   author's photo

anyone wants to get on or off. The buses are also desperately crowded.

Fortunately, there are many signs that the quality of life in these settlements improves through time. On my first visit to Casablanca, in 1978, most streets lacked drains and all but one street lacked paving. On my most recent visit in 1992, these problems had been largely resolved and many of the houses were solid two-storey structures. Perhaps the most ostentatious sign of progress, was the large satellite dish that had been installed in the settlement to receive television programmes from abroad. While Casablanca is still a poor settlement, it shows that some kind of improvement can take place.

Bogotá certainly does not give the impression that it is in decline. Of course, it escaped lightly from the regional debt crisis of the 1980s; the Colombian economy actually grew during the decade. More factories were built, more private banks and insurance offices were established, the number of government employees continued to grow, and the number of middle-class households increased greatly. The physical fabric of the city reflected this growth. More and more roads were paved, and the electricity and water systems spread outwards to supply the ever expanding suburban sprawl. There were many more cars on the road, and more and better buses. More skyscrapers and hotels appeared as well as shopping malls, cinemas and entertainment complexes. Every year Bogotá looked more and more like a North American city. The shift from the Spanish colonial churches and patio houses of Candelaria in the centre to the ugly Búlevar Niza shopping mall encapsulated the dominant trend.

At the same time, the sprawl of self-help suburbia is a reminder that Bogotá is an extraordinarily unequal place and that it faces some severe problems. Years of complaints about the appalling pollution in the River Bogotá have produced little improvement. The authorities considered building a sewage treatment plant too expensive, and the low-income settlements and villages downstream from Bogotá bear the terrible scar of that pollution. Only now is a project being planned with the World Bank to address the problem. In 1992 the electricity system failed the city. A combination of drought, administrative incompetence, and a measure of corruption meant that Bogotá, along with the rest of the country, was plunged into darkness every evening of the week. In April, most areas of the city were suffering from seven hours of power cuts a day. For people unused to candles and addicted to their favourite television soaps, it came as a terrible shock. Despite economic growth, progress in Bogotá has a habit of being constantly interrupted.

Bogotá is undoubtedly a crime-ridden and violent city. Petty crime, which has always been rife, is currently rampant and rates of car-jacking, armed robbery and kidnapping have recently escalated. Few homes, even in the low-income settlements, fail to take elaborate precautions against burglary. Higher-income families long ago started moving into estates with armed security guards or into high-rise apartment blocks. In the first eight months of 1993, 5,600 people in the city died violent deaths, and 2,000 of these were shot. The capital city has now overtaken Medellín as the most violent city in Colombia. Nationally, Colombia's murder rate in 1992 stood at 86 per 100,000 population, compared to 9 per 100,000 in the US. Perhaps the influence of drugs is partially responsible, although few people in Bogotá use cocaine or *basuco* - the local equivalent of crack. Insofar as a drug culture is evident in Bogotá, it is reflected most clearly in the increasing numbers of Mercedes and BMW cars on the streets.

Caracas

Caracas is undeniably a spectacular city. The drama begins on the journey from the airport. From Maiquetía, which is virtually on the beach, a modern motorway winds its way 17 miles to Venezuela's capital nestling in a narrow valley 3,000 feet up in the mountains. The motorway sweeps across deep ravines and through long tunnels in the hillside. Soon after leaving the airport, the passenger becomes aware of one of Caracas' dominant features; the *ranchos* or shanty towns clinging onto the slopes of the mountains. As

Caracas: building the Parque Central complex   author's photo

the city gets closer, more shanties crowd in on both sides. On leaving the last tunnel, they seem to be everywhere. As the road drops into the valley a different kind of modernist vision begins to unfold, with a skyline full of hundreds of skyscrapers. In central Caracas, everything seems to be in the air: mountains, apartment buildings, office blocks, advertising hoardings, even the slums!

Caracas has more skyscrapers than any other Latin American city, certainly than any other city of its size. Because it is located in a series of narrow valleys it is densely populated. Running through the valleys are the motorways which, together with the skyscrapers and the *ranchos*, most symbolise the city. Caracas was built on oil and a motorcar culture. The city needed motorways for the huge vehicles that every *caraqueño* was determined to drive. Easy money from the oilwells meant more and more motorways. More oil meant more money, more money meant more cars, more cars meant more motorways, and as more motorways would not fit in the narrow valleys, more cars meant more congestion. No-one could get to work. Despite the motorways, congestion is worse in few other Latin American cities. Only when the underground began operations in 1983 did the situation begin to improve a little.

The motorways both created and destroyed Caracas. Nowhere in the rest of Latin America is the old city centre so insignificant. Apart from the Plaza Bolívar and the Congress building, there are few traces of the colonial past. The centre of gravity long ago moved along the motorways to the commercial and business sub-centres which developed along the floor of the main valley: Sabana Grande, Chacaito, Chuao and Petare.

In Caracas, oil wealth flowed into motorways and skyscrapers, into expensive real estate and into public projects. In the process, it also built a series of spectacular follies. Perched far above the city is the empty Humboldt Hotel - a testament to *caraqueño* dreams of greatness, devised to house visitors who could only get to the hotel by cable-car. Then there is the *helicoide*, a commercial-cum-exhibition centre, which was never completed or used. In the 1950s, huge superblocks were built to house the poor. The country's autocratic leader, Marcos Pérez Jiménez, had declared a war on the *ranchos* and sent his troops to clear out the shanty towns. He thought that the slums created a bad public image, that the people of a modern capital should live in proper accommodation - even if they had no wish to be relocated. Arguably, the Parque Central complex is also a folly. A vast housing and office complex less than one mile from the Plaza Bolívar, it was intended for poor families close to the central city. Those families would be subsidised by selling the more expensive apartments to higher-income households who would pay the market price for their homes. Unfortunately, corruption and incompetence pushed up the costs of construction so that the expensive apartments could only be sold if subsidised. A former mayor of the city fled to Miami in the wake of the scandal.

Among the modern structures perhaps only the underground is really a sign of progress. It is clean, cheap, comfortable and the trains run on time. It is an oasis of efficiency in a desert of corruption and incompetence. It is also a dangerous mirage of the future. No-one knows how much it cost to build or how many fortunes were made in its construction. In the current economic environment, there is little chance that many more lines will be added to the system. And yet *caraqueños* are proud of it. Nothing, they argue, should ever again be built above ground; the only thing that works in Caracas is subterranean.

If oil was turned into real estate, and even put back under the ground, it was also transformed into slums. Not that much was spent on the slums beyond basic standpipes and electricity lines and the occasional attempt at demolition. But the promise of jobs attracted swarms of migrants from the countryside. In 1941, Caracas had little more than 300,000 people, twenty years later it had 1.3 million. The immigrant population needed somewhere to live and people did what they had done for generations in the countryside: they built their own homes. Between 1945 and 1948 when, after 120 years of independence, Venezuela had its first experience of democratic government, the population invaded public land on the hillsides. Since the slopes were too steep or too unstable to support skyscrapers, the authorities did little to oppose the occupations.

If Caracas is spectacular, it is not just because government extravagance turned the city into a concrete jungle of skyscrapers and motorways. It is also because the oil bonanza turned it into such an unequal place. The poor of Caracas are certainly not as poor as those of La Paz or Lima, but few would deny that the feel of poverty is exaggerated by the physical proximity of skyscraper and slum. Perhaps only in Rio de Janeiro's Copacabana district does poverty pose such a dramatic counterpoint to extreme affluence.

In part, Caracas is also too much like a North American city. It is too dependent on the car and, until recently, lacked decent public transport; it has been obsessed with large-scale building projects; it has failed to levy sufficient taxes on its inhabitants. Like most North American cities, it has its impressive buildings, both public and private. The Parque Central, the new Teresa Cedeño Theatre, the Central University, the Hilton, Tamanaco and, even, the Humboldt Hotels. What it lacks is a public conscience to keep it in order and to provide its people with decent services.

What makes Caracas tolerable is that it is also very much a Caribbean city. Whereas highland Bogotá goes to sleep at night, Caracas never quite closes its eyes. Caracas is undeniably lively, its people voluble, friendly, and brash. Much is done for show, few people ever save. Even during the recent recession, few restaurants were ever empty; *caraqueños* spent as if there were no economic downturn. The cars looked a little older but everyone kept driving. In the restaurants the sound level was increased by the frenzied ringing of portable phones, carried by seemingly every male diner.

Caracas should have had everything. At 3,000 feet the climate is delightful, warm yet not oppressive. Half an hour away is the Caribbean, with a series of spectacular beaches waiting for the *caraqueños* to come and play. The picturesque valleys with their mountain backcloth offer a most attractive locale for Venezuela's capital. With oil funding its future, one government after another sought to embellish the national capital. They employed foreign technicians and planners. They spent lavishly on motorways, office complexes, apartment blocks and underground railways. In the 1940s, a great new government complex was created in the centre of the city at the terminus of one of the city's major motorways. Urban renovation removed slums and built new roads, bus stations and public buildings. With so many good intentions and so much money, what could possibly go wrong?

In the event, a great deal. Corruption, inefficiency, totalitarian rule, an excess of populism and the misuse of modern technology were fuelled by oil wealth to produce a parody of urban utopia. The accoutrements of modernity were present, indeed everything was modern, but there was little spirit of community. Those with power took all they could, those without power received very little. Planning should have removed disorder; in Caracas it managed to aggravate it.

Guadalajara

By Mexican standards, Guadalajara is both a very pretty and well-ordered city. There is little here to compare with the squalor and disorder of either Mexico City or Monterrey. The City of Roses is proud of its reputation and does its best to sustain the image. It has long maintained an enviable community spirit, with the business community investing in public projects to improve the look and the feel of the city. Over the years, such collaboration has provided Guadalajara with infrastructure and services. It has led to the ordered development of the western suburbs and the construction of large numbers of squares, fountains and public monuments. Many of the city's main streets are lined with trees.

Although it grew quickly after 1940, Guadalajara managed to maintain much of its original character. In Tlaquepaque, until recently a separate town, visitors can wander through a pedestrianised complex of artisan shops which successfully combine the better side of commercialism with the feel of a well-run museum. In the central square, they can eat and

Guadalajara: Tlaquepaque square

drink serenaded by *mariachi* music.

Even the central city has been kept alive through imaginative public projects. Threatened with traffic congestion in the 1940s, the authorities responded by widening the streets and remodelling the area around the cathedral. Four major squares surround the cathedral, forming the shape of a cross. More recently, efforts to resurrect commercial life in the centre have produced a huge new shopping precinct. Around a series of squares, giant statues and fountains, some of Mexico's major stores ply their trade. The vast Plaza Tapatía is a testimony to imaginative architecture, combining modernity with tradition. Its fountains and walkways lead from modern department stores to the colonial jewel of the city, the Hospice of Cabañas. Few cities around the world have managed to combine old with new quite so successfully.

Yet there are those who have always argued that Guadalajara's appearance of order and tranquillity is a façade, that Guadalajara looks neat and tidy because it hides its underbelly. Critics claim that shanty towns did not spread in Guadalajara in the way they did elsewhere, because the authorities did not permit their development. It was not that poverty was any less of a problem, merely that it was less visible. The industrial structure of Guadalajara managed to hide a substructure of small workshops. Until transnational corporations began to establish themselves in the city in the

1960s, Guadalajara had little large-scale industry and was a centre of small-and medium-scale plants. There was not a large working class as in Monterrey, but rather a majority of artisans and small businessmen, who were often just as poor.

The lid began to come off the pot during the 1940s when shanty towns began to grow. Officially, these were legal developments which fulfilled the requirements of the first planning law of 1944 and its later revisions, and officially they were provided with services and infrastructure before the inhabitants moved in. In practice, the authorities did not check whether the settlements had services or not. If much of the planning was a charade, low-income settlement did develop less anarchically than in many other cities. Until 1970, the developers laid out settlements in ways similar to the design of middle-income settlements and even provided something in the way of services. After 1970, however, the process deteriorated seriously, and there was much less difference between the low-income suburbs of Guadalajara and those in most other Mexican cities. The plots became smaller, the services less generous, and the land sold increasingly belonged to rural communities (ejidos), whose heritage was gradually usurped by the rapidly expanding city.

The image of Guadalajara as a traditional Mexican city also began to change as North American transnationals flooded into the city in the 1960s. Important companies such as Kodak, Motorola, Ralston Purina, Sears, Celanese and Union Carbide chose Guadalajara because of its placid workforce, its pleasant climate and its desirable urban image. But in the process of locating in western Mexico, they began to change it. Guadalajara's population grew rapidly from 240,000 in 1940, to 812,000 in 1960 and 2,193,000 in 1980. Its suburbs began to sprawl as the number of buses and cars increased.

By the 1980s, large parts of Guadalajara were looking more and more like a North American city. Nowhere was this more true than in the affluent southwest of the city where new hotels were opened and a major new shopping complex was created - the Plaza del Sol. Here the Hyatt Hotel stands close to McDonalds, surrounded by hundreds of parking lots.

Less affluent parts of Guadalajara also began to look more like other Mexican cities with their vast shanty towns and deficient services. In the 1980s, unemployment began to rise as the recession hit even the less vulnerable Guadalajara economy. More people began to leave the city for the United States, and more became involved in drug trafficking as cocaine passed through Guadalajara on its way north. The city which had hidden its poverty for so long was visibly managing less well during the severe Mexican recession.

The image of the city has also suffered recently from two traumatic events. By far the most serious was the massive explosion of 22 April 1992 that killed some 200 people and tore out 26 blocks from one of the city's central districts. The petrol vapour which escaped from the local PEMEX refinery into the central sewerage network was a tragic consequence of incompetence and neglect (see p.124). On 24 May 1993 a further dent to Guadalajara's image came in the form of a dramatic shootout between drug traffickers outside the airport. Killed in the crossfire were a Roman Catholic cardinal and six other people.

Rio de Janeiro

Rio de Janeiro is one of the most famous cities in the world. It is spectacularly blessed with a fabulous natural backcloth of mountains and sea. Everyone recognises pictures of the Corcovado, with its statue of Christ, and the Sugar Loaf mountain rising out of the yacht-strewn Guanabara Bay. The locals joke and say that God worked hard to create Rio and did such a good job that he decided that it was not fair on the rest of the world. So, to even things up, he created the *carioca*, the inhabitant of Rio de Janeiro.

Despite such self-deprecating humour, *carioca* culture has made its mark by giving the world samba, carnival, the Maracana football stadium and the Girl from Ipanema. More than any other Latin American city, Rio oozes life and glamour. With its alluring mixture of climate, sea, mountains, glitz and geniality, it should be the most perfect place to live. For the rich living in the south of the city, it possibly is.

The affluent live close to the beaches, isolated from the rest of the city by the mountains which are penetrated only by expensively constructed tunnels. While these affluent households live at surprisingly high urban densities, the price they pay for property suggests that they consider crowding a minor inconvenience compared to the pleasures of living near the beaches.

Unfortunately, most of Rio's inhabitants live in much more humble surroundings. For, despite its glamorous image, Rio is a very unequal place. Indeed, in 1989, it was by far the most unequal of Brazil's largest nine cities, with one-third of its population living below the poverty line.

Most of the poor live far away either in the Baixada Fluminense, a vast urban sprawl twenty or so miles to the north of the city or in the western suburbs even further out. Not only is most of the population poor, but their homes are very poorly serviced. In Nova Iguaçu, a huge self-help city to the north of the city, less than two-fifths of the population had running water in 1980, and seven-tenths lacked a sewage system. With a population of some 1.5 million, this vast suburb had only 265 doctors and 27 dentists. Nova Iguaçu is typical of the swampy Baixada Fluminense, an area that was occupied rapidly after 1950 when land prices rose dramatically in the south of the city. Not only are such districts poorly serviced, but they are

Rio de Janeiro: a mansion with a view

author's photo

MASSACRE IN THE FAVELA

It was a few minutes before midnight. Jane da Silva Santos, 56 years old, had spent the Sunday looking after her husband, retired bricklayer Gilberto dos Santos, 61 years old. She had only left him for half an hour to go with the rest of the family to the *favela's* church.

In the connecting rooms of the house were crowded the couple's five children, aged between 15 and 27, their daughter-in-law, Rubia, and five grandchildren aged from one month to ten years.

When they heard the first shots, they all thought that it must be one of the frequent shoot-outs between the military police and the drug traffickers who ran the Vigario Geral *favela*. When the sound of a rifle shot shook the house and the door opened, Rubia ran white-faced into the room with the baby in her arms.

Some 15 hooded men entered the house clutching smoking guns and shouting: "We want to drink blood". Jane hugged her daughter-in-law and both knelt begging for mercy, until they fell riddled with bullets. Gilberto sat up in bed only to sag backwards with a bullet through his forehead. The only survivor, a grandchild of one year, was crying next to the body of her mother when the killers went into the other room to finish off the children of the couple.

Immediately afterwards the men crossed the street and entered the modest bar of Joacir Medeiros, a retired man of 60 years. Eight neighbours were drinking beer, talking happily about the victory of Brazil's national football team over Bolivia earlier that day.

The hooded men asked if they were workers and demanded to see their documents. They did not look at them, throwing them on the floor. They dropped a tear-gas bomb and then started firing until no-one was left on their feet. Only two people survived by pretending that they were dead.

In total, around fifty masked men - soldiers from the military police - killed 21 inhabitants of Vigario Geral, a working-class neighbourhood that was first established in 1961.

Its 30,000 inhabitants now feel terrorised by threats of further violence.

Ricardo Sosa, *El Espectador*, 3 September 1993.

also a long way from the centre of the city; most commuters face daily round trips of two or three hours. Life in this area is harsh. A recessionary environment means that levels of un-and under-employment here are very high. Life is also very unhealthy because of the poor water and sanitation system. This is best reflected in the appallingly high figures for infant mortality; 90 out of every 1,000 babies die in this area every year.

Unfortunately, there is little sign of improvement in the position of the poor; recession and inflation in recent years have worsened their lives. Certainly, social conditions have deteriorated badly in recent years. In the process, Rio has also developed an unenviable reputation for drugs, crime and violence, and is regularly portrayed in the international media as the city which most suffers from death squads. During the 1970s para-military groups eliminated political opponents, while today they are more likely to kill some of the city's many street children or the inhabitants of the *favelas*.

The problems of poverty and recession are shared by every city in Brazil, but Rio de Janeiro has also been suffering a relative decline. It became Brazil's national capital in 1763, but lost its position in 1960 when the utopia of Brasília was constructed. It was Brazil's largest city until the 1960s, but its 9.6 million people now pale into relative insignificance when matched against the 15.2 million of its much larger southeastern 'neighbour', São Paulo. Its population is now growing at less than one per cent per annum. In economic terms, Rio's prominence has waned even more quickly. It has lost out to other Brazilian cities in terms of both industrial and government jobs and in the political struggle for resources. Even its tourist business is facing severe problems. In the 1980s it received up to half a million tourists a year, between 1987 and 1990, however, the total number of visitors to Brazil fell by half and those to Rio by 62 per cent.[1]

Of course, it would be stretching the imagination to pretend that Rio de Janeiro is finished. Its attractions still mean that many transnational corporations prefer to locate their offices there. Several state enterprises have also withstood the commercial and administrative allure of São Paulo and Brasília for the pleasures of Rio. Recently, the telecommunications company has also agreed to establish a major new satellite technology system in the city.

The local administration is also trying to do something about rescuing Rio from the wave of drug-related attacks on tourists and human rights abuses. A new left-wing mayor, César Maia of the Democratic Movement party, has established a special force of unarmed municipal guards and has attempted to convince the state authorities to crack down on leading drug traffickers and some top policemen.

It is to be hoped that such initiatives are successful for, if they are not, there is a real threat hanging over Rio's place in the sun.

La Paz [2]

La Paz is a dramatic city, unlike any other major urban area in appearance. From the air it looks like an inclined wide-lipped oval bowl; running along much of its base is a seam, or ridge - a line of skyscrapers comprising the modern downtown area. Two-thirds of La Paz's population of 800,000 live within the bowl and up the sides, with upper-class neighbourhoods at the lowest point. The top edge of the bowl, El Alto, is part of the Altiplano Plateau and the site of mixed low-income residential and industrial uses. The city is given additional character by the nearby majestic mountain, Illimani, which looks over it from a height of more than 20,400 feet.

La Paz is Bolivia's capital and largest city. It produces more than half of the gross national product and provides 45 percent of the nation's employment in the industrial sector. Yet only about a third of La Paz's economically active population work in the industrial sector, and of these less than a quarter work in companies with more than twenty employees. The rest make their living as artisans and in small-scale businesses. The top fifth of the income scale earns 65 per cent of all income while the lowest fifth earns less than 3 per cent.

About a third of the people of La Paz are Indians who have come from small communities of the Altiplano, bringing with them their distinctive Aymara language and culture, dress and customs. The migrants maintain close ties to the countryside. Almost three-quarters of the migrants return to their place of origin at least once a year. More than any other major city of Latin America, La Paz is a meeting place for indigenous and European cultures, and much of the transition from one to the other is made in the downtown tenements and *barrios*.

The people of La Paz are for the most part poor. A series of devaluations beginning in February 1982 caused household income to deteriorate in dollar terms. By April 1983, average monthly household income was worth only US$40. Artisans faced increasing hardships as the prices of imported raw materials, tools, and machinery skyrocketed while the demand for their services decreased. Families consumed less and less of relatively costly foods, such as meat and eggs, and more of the staples of the Andean diet, principally potatoes. By the middle of 1983 the effects of a countrywide drought were felt in La Paz as increasing numbers of non-Spanish-speaking highland peasants appeared along the sidewalks in the centre of the city awkwardly asking for humiliating, but necessary, hand outs.

Housing is important to the people of La Paz both as shelter and as

La Paz: View from El Alto   Phillip Edwards/PANOS Pictures

a symbol. The climate of La Paz is often inclement, with heavy rains from November to March, temperatures below freezing, and cold winds on the hillsides and the Altiplano where most of the poor live. Houses in La Paz need a sturdy exterior. Building material is often adobe, with roofs of corrugated aluminium. The shacks of plywood, cardboard, and odd bits of refuse found in many cities of other Latin American countries are not in evidence in La Paz.

Because of the steep inclines of La Paz, much of the land is subject to floods and landslides. This helps explain why more than a third of all houses are not connected to piped water. In low-income areas this figure jumps to 86 percent. More than three-quarters of the people in these areas get their water from public taps. More than one in ten families in the poor neighbourhoods get their water from generally unsanitary sources such as rivers, drainage ditches, and stagnant pools. A third of the city's population has no sewer connection. In the poor areas of the city, this figure rise to 89 per cent. Electricity, however, is well provided, with only 14 percent lacking it citywide.

In the southwestern portion of the bowl of La Paz, about three-quarters up from the base to the top, is the neighbourhood of *8 de diciembre*. It is part of the larger region of Sopocachi, a venerable, staid community of middle- and upper-class families. The *8 de diciembre* is separated from its elegant neighbour by the Cotahuma River, a foul-smelling running latrine and open garbage pit bordering the settlement on the north and east. The river frequently floods and changes its course, spreading filth and causing the area to be badly suited for construction.

Despite its disadvantages the residents consider it a most pleasant and convenient place to live. Adjacent to one of the most desirable residential neighbourhoods of La Paz, it is only a half hour by foot and 15 minutes by bus from downtown. In addition, the community has an excellent view of Illimani across the bowl to the east.

The new urban settlement was founded on April 18, 1965. By naming their community after the Roman Catholic Feast of the Immaculate Conception, which is celebrated as a local religious holiday in Sopocachi, the early residents were not only demonstrating their faith but forging a desired link with the prestigious community of Sopocachi.

By mid-1983 there was little meat to be found on the tables of *8 de diciembre* residents, and many men had to replace beer with the cheaper but more injurious local grain alcohol (*chicha*). Because families were large and poor, houses tended to be more crowded (than in the rest of the city); an average of 5.7 persons per family and 3.0 persons per room. The high internal densities and lack of urban services, together with the high altitude and sometimes harsh climate, had adversely affected the health of area residents. Child mortality was high; 22 of the 106 children born in the five years preceding the survey had died.

* * * * * * * * * * * *

Rio de Janeiro does not feel much like Bogotá or Caracas, nor Guadalajara much like La Paz. Altitude, climate, people and culture are very different in each. There are, of course, important similarities, most obviously as one visits the wealthier areas of these cities. Everywhere the housing of the rich is ostentatiously attractive and their shopping areas contain fancy boutiques, wine stores and supermarkets. The business centres also look alike with their high-rise office blocks and expensive hotels.

Poorer residential areas, on the other hand, look more disparate. Whereas the poor can live in flimsy accommodation in the warmth of Rio, they need more solid shelter to survive the chill nights of Bogotá or La Paz. The wooden *favelas* find their parallel in the brick-built shanty town dwellings of Bogotá or La Paz. But one thing is shared; few visitors will leave the low-income areas of any of the cities in any doubt that the people living there are desperately poor. The poor have clearly been forced to build their own shelter and the smell betrays the fact that far too many homes lack any connection to the main sewer. The run-down state of the electricity system is revealed by the tangled wires hanging from most of the lampposts, for in the face of official neglect the poor steal their electricity.

The five cities are also similar in their familiar concoction of urban ills. Too many cars and too little public transport; too much pollution and too few decent jobs; too many public officials and too little competent administration. All these cities have grown extremely rapidly during the last half century and in the process have developed a heady brew of social problems. If the combined forces of economic recession and falling rates of fertility have recently slowed the pace of urban growth, that has only provided limited relief for the urban authorities. After all, they still have to cope with too much poverty with too few resources.

It is these similarities which justify the writing of this book. If the actual differences between cities tend to weaken the concept of a typical Latin American city, there is nevertheless something that makes the region's cities distinctive from most cities elsewhere. The common bond comes partly from language (although that does not really apply to Brazil), and partly from a common history and the strong cultural roots that were laid during almost three hundred years of Iberian rule. The link also comes from the broadly similar level of development across the region; for while Latin American cities are much more affluent than those in most of Africa and Asia, they are much poorer than most in Western Europe or North America. The parallels also derive from the extreme inequality that characterises all of the region's cities bar those of Cuba. Whatever the precise cause, there is a quality and distinctiveness about the Latin American city that needs to be explained and understood. The rest of the book is dedicated to that task.

Notes

(1) Cited by del Rio (1992:271).

(2) This section is an abridged version of Salmen (1987:15-21).

Further reading

Bogotá: Gilbert (1978), Santana   (1989), Silva (1992)and Suárez (ed.) (1990).

Caracas: Morris (1978), Myers (1978), Ovalles and Córdoba (1986), Perna (1981) and Ray (1969).

Guadalajara: Alba (1986), Arias and Roberts (1985), Gilbert and Varley (1991), Morfín and Sánchez (1984), Vázquez (1989), Walton (1978) and Wario (1984).

Rio de Janeiro: Gilbert (1988), Mainwaring (1989), Câmara (1991), Perlman (1976) and Tolosa (1992).

La Paz: Beijaard (1992), Salmen (1987) and van Lindert (1991).

2

THE GROWTH OF THE LATIN AMERICAN CITY

Back in time

The Latin American city is very old. The Aztecs, Mayas and Incas had all created impressive urban forms as much as a thousand years before the Iberian invasions of the sixteenth century. The remains of Cuzco in Peru, Tiahuanuco in Bolivia and Monte Albán, Tenochtitlán, Teotihuacán and Xochicalco in Mexico are eloquent testimony to the presence of urban civilisations well before the arrival of Europeans.

This pre-Columbian heritage is almost completely absent from the contemporary urban scene because the Spanish demolished the indigenous cities that they found. While they used the capital of the Sun God as foundations for the new city of Cuzco, elsewhere few remains are visible. Conquest meant the building of new cities, indeed whole new urban systems. Together with the Portuguese in colonial Brazil, the Spanish constructed an intricate administrative system based on a well-connected network of new towns and cities. As Jorge Hardoy (1975:25) points out: "This spatial structure constitutes the basis of the present-day scheme of continental urbanization." Most of today's cities were founded by the Spanish or the Portuguese during the sixteen and seventeenth centuries.[1]

The Portuguese and Spanish Empires were run from the cities which were centres of conquest and administration rather than market places. According to Fernando Henrique Cardoso (1975:169):

> The city that dotted the Iberian empire in the Americas, Lusitanian as well as Hispanic, was more a city of officials than a city of burghers. Neither the market nor local councils had the power to oppose the King's courts, colonial regulations, and the interests of the Crown, or to resist the colonial exploitation that cast Iberian royalty and bourgeoisie into the rigid mold of mercantile capitalism. At the opposite pole was the owner of land,

Pre-colonial urbanisation:Teotihuacan author's photo

Indians, or slaves. The official and the lord were the social types that gave life to the cities.

While some of the erstwhile 'giants' of the Spanish and Portuguese urban systems are now merely small towns, most of the really important administrative centres developed into today's major cities. Lima and Mexico City, the capitals of the viceroyalties of Peru and New Spain, retain an all-dominant position within their modern national boundaries.[2] Similarly, nearly all of the twenty current capital cities were key administrative centres during the colonial period. In this sense, Latin America's urban system is rather old.

Similarly, the past is responsible for an important ingredient in the design of today's city. Both the Spaniards and the Portuguese laid out their cities according to a set plan based on practice at home. While the Portuguese were much less rigorous in their planning and allowed more local variation than did the Spanish, the influence of the colonial city is clearly recognisable throughout the region. The central square, around which were located the church or cathedral, the main administrative offices and the homes of the elite, remains at the centre of most Latin American cities. Equally, the grid-iron street plan which spreads out from the central square remains, topography permitting, the basis of most modern road layouts (see Figure 2.1).

Figure 2.1
Plan of Santo Domingo

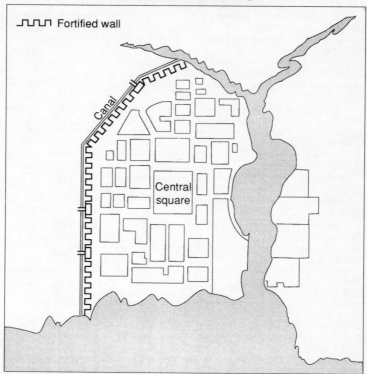

Source: Recreated from *Montanus Arnoldus,* De Nieuwe en Onbekende Weerld
(Amsterdam 1691)

But, if the Latin American city is in one sense very old, it is very new
in another. In 1900, most Latin Americans lived in the countryside and only
three cities had more than half a million inhabitants. By 1930, the total urban
population of the whole region had still not reached 20 million. By
comparison with Mexico City's current population of around 18 million and
the present Latin American urban total of some 300 million, the 1930 total
pales into insignificance. Even by 1950, there were still only six cities -
Buenos Aires, Lima, Mexico City, Rio de Janeiro, Santiago and São Paulo
- with more than a million people; today, there are arguably 39 (see Table
2.4). The speed of urban growth in Latin America in recent years is
undoubtedly very impressive.

Table 2.1
Urban population (per cent) in Latin America, 1940-90

COUNTRY	1940	1960	1980	1990
ARGENTINA	na	74	83	86
BOLIVIA	na	24	33	51
BRAZIL	31	46	64	75
CHILE	52	68	82	86
COLOMBIA	29	53	68	70
CUBA	46	55	65	75
ECUADOR	na	36	44	56
MEXICO	35	51	66	73
PERU	35	47	65	70
VENEZUELA	31	63	79	91
LATIN AMERICA	33	44	64	72

Urban population is defined as those living in settlements of more than 20,000 inhabitants
Source: Wilkie *et al.* (1990)

Urbanisation is also new in the sense that the look and shape of the cities have been greatly modified. While the central square and the grid-iron street plan can still be seen in most large cities, and while they still dominate smaller urban places, the bus, the car, the skyscraper and improved forms of electricity and water provision have transformed the city over the last fifty years. Add large-scale industrial development to the recipe and it is clear that in many respects the form of the Latin American city is very new.

From a rural to an urban society

Until comparatively recently, most people lived in the countryside. Only Argentina, Chile, Cuba and Uruguay contained an urban majority in 1950 and as Table 2.1 shows, less than one-half of Latin Americans in 1960 lived in urban areas.

Since 1940, of course, urbanisation has been rapid and in a period of fifty years Latin America has been transformed. While the numbers of people living in rural areas has only recently begun to fall in absolute terms, the proportion of rural inhabitants has been in constant decline. As a result of cityward migration, most Latin American cities have grown extremely quickly and, for short periods at least, some have grown at quite spectacular rates. During the 1940s, for example, Caracas grew by 7.6 per cent annually, Cali by 8 per cent and São Paulo by 7.4 per cent; during the 1950s, Guadalajara grew annually by 6.7 per cent. If these percentage figures are insufficiently impressive, during the 1970s Mexico City's population increased by 5.1 million people and that of São Paulo by 4.0 million.

Latin America was transformed from a rural to an urban region by a combination of falling mortality rates, rapid internal migration, economic development and changing technology. In 1930, Latin America had just over 100 million inhabitants; sixty years later, its population had passed the 425 million mark. Control of the worst diseases such as malaria, the introduction of drugs to treat pneumonia and tuberculosis, and immunisation campaigns against widespread killers such as measles, diptheria and typhoid led to a spectacular decline in mortality rates. Average life expectancy almost doubled from an average of 34 years in 1930 to 65 years by the early 1980s.

With death rates plummeting, fertility continued at a very high level in most of the region. Excluding Argentina and Uruguay, where average birth rates per thousand population were in the low 20s, fertility rates in the 1960s averaged around 45. It was not until the 1970s and 1980s that fertility rates in most of the region began to fall substantially, with average birth rates dropping from 42 per thousand in the early 1960s to 33 per thousand in the early 1980s and 27 per thousand in the early 1990s. In the meantime, Latin America's population boomed.

There is a clear link between rates of urban growth and national population growth. Argentina became an urban country at the turn of the century as immigration from Europe boosted its population. Similar patterns of growth occurred in Uruguay and southern Brazil around the same time. Elsewhere, rapid urbanisation only took place when mortality rates began to decline during the 1940s and 1950s. With fertility remaining high, rural populations began to increase and people began to move to the cities in large numbers. As Table 2.2 shows, it was only in the 1970s that population growth began to slow in most countries.

Since most of the population were living in the countryside, it was the rural areas which bore the brunt of the increase. Rapid growth created a problem insofar as Latin America's land tenure system was very unequal and few families had ever had sufficient land to feed their children. Although rural populations continued to grow in absolute terms up to the 1970s, huge numbers moved to the cities.

Table 2.2
National population growth rates, 1920-75

COUNTRY	1920-25	1930-35	1940-45	1950-55	1960-65	1970-75
ARGENTINA	3.2	1.9	1.7	2.1	1.6	1.3
BRAZIL	2.1	2.1	2.3	3.0	2.9	2.6
CHILE	1.5	1.6	1.5	2.4	2.5	1.7
COLOMBIA	1.9	2.0	2.4	3.1	3.3	2.2
ECUADOR	1.1	1.7	2.1	2.8	3.6	2.9
MEXICO	1.0	1.8	2.9	2.9	3.5	3.2
PERU	1.5	1.7	1.8	2.0	3.1	2.7
VENEZUELA	1.9	2.3	2.8	4.0	3.3	3.6
LATIN AMERICA	1.9	1.9	2.2	2.7	2.9	2.6

Source: Wilkie *et al.* (1988:109)

That the cities could absorb this flood of migrants was due to economic growth. While jobs were always scarce, the absolute increase in urban employment was impressive. In places, manufacturing jobs increased rapidly. In Mexico City, the number of industrial jobs grew from 271,000 in 1950 to 477,000 in 1960 and 698,000 in 1970. Commerce and finance expanded enormously, creating a whole range of new jobs for shop assistants, street vendors, bank clerks and insurance workers. More people were also absorbed by the growing public sector. Whether or not they were all productively employed, the numbers of school teachers, bureaucrats, health workers, street cleaners and electricity workers increased dramatically. If far too many newcomers were required to work for very low pay, few were unemployed and even fewer were worse off than if they had stayed in the countryside.

While the expansion of employment helped absorb the newcomers, new forms of technology helped to house them. The introduction of bricks, cement, concrete blocks and new kinds of roofing eased the process of urban expansion, even for the majority who were increasingly living in self-help housing. New forms of transportation allowed the development of suburban housing. Despite the fast rate of urban growth, the population was kept

Cultural colonialism: cinema complex in Guadalajara   author's photo

relatively healthy; few cities suffered from the epidemics that had plagued urban life in the early twentieth century.[3] If living conditions were often squalid, they were no worse than conditions in the countryside. And, unlike the rural situation, economic growth promised to gradually improve the quality of urban life.

The shape of the city

As I argued in Chapter One, Latin America's cities share many common features. Buenos Aires and Mexico City are very much larger and more sophisticated than Asunción or Tegucigalpa, but notwithstanding variations caused by differences in climate and relief, what is surprising about Latin America is how similar its cities look.

Several factors lie behind this apparent uniformity. Not only were their colonial cores built to a similar urban plan, but the processes directing their subsequent expansion have also been remarkably similar. First, every Latin American country has long formed part of the international production system. Indeed, as industrialisation, foreign investment, the commercialisation of agriculture, technological adaptation and alien cultural practices have swept through the region, its cities have naturally taken on a similar look, not only to one another, but also to those of the principal source of new technology, investment and culture: North America. The transnationalisation of production and technology influenced the development of urban employment and production structures. Differences are apparent but, apart from the writing on the signs, it is sometimes difficult to distinguish the streets of Caracas from those of Los Angeles, those of São Paulo from those of New York.

Second, most Latin American countries have followed a similar kind of development path. From the sixteenth century to the middle of the twentieth, every country relied principally on mineral or agricultural exports to sustain its economy. From the 1930s every country began to industrialise, protecting itself carefully behind high tariff walls and complicated import-licence schemes. From the 1940s to the late 1970s, import-substituting industrialisation produced slow but sustained economic development. During the 1980s, practically every economy was affected badly by the debt crisis which led to a decline in per capita income in all but a handful of countries.

Third, common forms of urban development are due to the increasing internationalisation of consumer tastes. Latin America's affluent suburbs featured English-style housing during the 1940s and California-style housing during the 1950s and 1960s. Today, most elite residential areas feel much like North American suburbs. Indeed, the whole suburban life-style is increasingly imitative of the United States, based on the car and its associated retail structures such as the supermarket and shopping and entertainment malls. Bogotá's Unicentro and Guadalajara's Plaza del Sol shopping centres are almost pure North American transplants. Even the restaurants are the same: McDonald's, Denny's and Kentucky Fried Chicken. Latin America's self-help suburbia has also adopted international consumer goods from Coca-Cola to designer labels and personal stereos. Television has helped to modify Latin American life by bringing Dallas, Dynasty, Michael Jackson and Madonna into most front rooms. As a result, it has changed cultural expectations and stimulated new consumer tastes. It is estimated that in 1986 there were 26 million television sets in Brazil and 9.5 million in Mexico, the vast bulk in the urban areas.

Finally, Latin American cities are similar insofar as there is insufficient well-paid employment. As a result, large numbers of people in every city eke out a living in some part of the so-called 'informal sector'. The consequences of low pay, albeit usually much higher than rural incomes, are obvious in the dress, retail outlets and housing of the majority. Every Latin American city is dominated by this mass of poor people and the contrast they make with the well-dressed, affluent minority. The colour of the faces of the poor may differ throughout the region, but their dress and work differ remarkably little. With the exception of Cuba, few governments have made a determined effort to rectify the inequalities in urban society. The divide between rich and poor remains great, and urban poverty casts a shadow across all of Latin America.

Economic development and urban growth

The period from 1940 to 1980 was both an intense phase of urban development and also a period of sustained economic growth throughout the region. When the economic crisis of the 1980s hit Latin America, urban growth began to slow. The nature of urban growth is integrally linked to the pace and form of economic development. Without understanding the link between the two, misleading conclusions may be drawn about the nature of the city.

First, urban growth has long contributed to economic development rather than acting as a drain on the economy. Since urban activities tend to be more productive than most rural activities, the shift from rural to urban production raised incomes. As a result, those moving to the city were less the victims of migration than its beneficiaries. They also contributed to economic development rather than creating a social problem which should have been stemmed at source.[4]

Table 2.3
Population growth of selected Latin American cities, 1960-1990

(per cent per annum)

CITY	1960s	1970s	1980s
MEXICO CITY	5.6	3.7	3.0
BOGOTA	6.2	4.1	3.2
CARACAS	5.0	1.7	1.2
SANTIAGO	4.2	2.9	2.4
BUENOS AIRES	2.1	1.8	1.5
SAO PAULO	5.5	4.1	3.7
RIO DE JANEIRO	3.7	2.2	2.2
LIMA	7.3	5.1	4.1

Source: United Nations, Department of International Economic and Social Affairs (1991) and national censuses.

POVERTY AND SOCIAL SPENDING IN MEXICO DURING THE 1980s

Mexico's crisis years (1982-89) further impoverished the population. During these years the country's poor grew in both absolute and relative terms. Per capita GDP fell 14 per cent, and the decline in earnings was very unevenly distributed. While the country's population expanded from 71.4 million in 1981 to 81.2 million in 1987, the country's poor grew from 32.1 to 41.3 million. In this brief six-year period, nine out of every ten Mexicans added to the national population were to be found in the ranks of the poor. Today forty-one million Mexicans are unable to satisfy their basic needs, and seventeen million live in extreme poverty.

The portion of GDP which corresponds to wage earnings, which had always been low in Mexico compared to more advanced countries, dropped from 36 per cent in 1980 to 28.6 per cent in 1986. Over the same period, unemployment rose from 6 to 12.1 per cent of the economically active population.

The state's role in promoting equality also deteriorated notably during these years, dropping at an even faster rate than the federal budget. From 1981 to 1988, the federal budget fell from 33.8 to 19.8 per cent of GDP. Government investment expenditures fell proportionately faster, from 11.2 per cent of GDP to 4.2 per cent. The cutback in government investment in rural development was calamitous, from 2.4 per cent to 0.2 per cent; investment in regional development went from 1.4 to 0.2 per cent of GDP; and public investment in the social sector fell from 3.3 to 0.3 per cent. Thus, while the total national budget fell 42.5 per cent with respect to GDP, these three investment categories fall by 92, 96, and 91 per cent respectively, in their share of GDP in 1981.

Source: Tello (1990: 58-9)

In terms of social conditions, several indicators point to the continued spread and entrenchment of poverty, and an unprecedented social debt. The long years of crisis had one primary effect on the education sector: reduced government spending. Spending on education declined in real terms from 1981 to 1987 and, as a percentage of GDP, was lower in 1987 than it had been in eleven years. A corollary effect of the crisis, with serious implications for education, is that household strategies for confronting economic hardship included the integration of children and adolescents into the labour market.

The declining investment in education halted construction of educational infrastructure, including classrooms and laboratories. Budget constraints also reduced the availability of free textbooks and increased the student-teacher ratio, even as overall enrolment levels fell.

During the 1980s Mexicans' nutritional levels nose-dived due to the surprisingly rapid drop in consumption of certain foods. People are eating less, and what they are eating is less nutritious. The decline in nutritional levels has multiple roots: a contracting job market and reduced household incomes; regressive tendencies in social spending; a fiscal policy characterized since 1982 by shrinking subsidies and increased prices for public goods and services; and lagging minimum-wage rates relative to prices for basic goods.

As household incomes decline, the percentage of the population that is limited to the most basic foodstuffs increases. But subsidies and other policies for ensuring that the poor can afford basic goods have been cut back or even eliminated, with clear - albeit indirect - implications for consumption.

Nutrition has a direct effect on health. Government health expenditures have not compensated the decline in health levels following from decreased levels of nutrition. The budgetary cutbacks necessitated by the crisis have led to an increased incidence of diseases that were previously thought to be under control or even eradicated. Particularly notable are recent accounts of diseases associated with extreme poverty, such as malaria, dengue fever, and other illnesses.

Source: Cordera and González (1990: 27-35)

Second, because urban growth occurred during periods of economic expansion, governments could raise taxes and provide services and infrastructure for the burgeoning cities. Had governments not been able to extend water and electricity systems, bus routes and health care, the urban situation would have become dire. As it was, Latin American cities absorbed huge numbers of new inhabitants with relative ease. The history of the Latin American city between 1940 and 1980 is one of continuous improvement, if not for everyone, at least for the bulk of the population.

The 1980s, of course, saw the reversal of what had been assumed to be normal practice. Between 1980 and 1989, the overall gross national product of Latin America and the Caribbean declined by 8.3 per cent. Among Latin American countries, only Chile, Colombia and Cuba managed to grow. Most of the rest experienced major recessions, with per capita income in Argentina, Ecuador, Peru and Venezuela declining by around one-quarter, and in Nicaragua by one-third. Not only did average incomes fall but the urban areas fared worse than the countryside. The cities suffered from rising unemployment as large numbers of industries went out of business because governments had reduced protection against imports and cut back on subsidies. Urban unemployment rose as governments laid off increasing numbers of workers. In some countries, urban unemployment rose to unprecedented levels: 20 per cent in Chile in 1982 and 22 per cent in Panama in 1989. The urban population also suffered as governments cut back on social expenditure. Social spending was severely reduced in most countries during the recession of the 1980s.

A clear consequence of the economic recession was a slowing in the pace of urban growth. The region's major cities grew much more slowly during the 1980s than they had previously.

Urban primacy and the growth of megacities

Despite the recent slowing of urban growth, Latin America still contains some of the world's largest metropolitan areas. However their urban areas are defined, Mexico City and São Paulo are certainly among the world's most populous cities. If forecasts that Mexico City will have 30 million people by the year 2000 seem hugely wide of the mark, its population is clearly going to reach 20 million.

When compared with Mexico City or São Paulo, most of the region's other cities are relatively small. But by the standards of many other parts of the world, even these smaller cities are rather impressive. Apart from Rio de Janeiro and Buenos Aires, which both have over ten million inhabitants, even Latin American cities which most readers will have difficulty placing on a map, have several million inhabitants. As Table 2.4 shows, Latin America now has 11 cities with more than 3 million inhabitants. The region has 39 cities with more than one million people, and no fewer than 14 of these are in Brazil.

Not only are the metropolitan centres of Latin America enormous, but in many cases they are very much larger than any other city in the same country. Thus Lima is approximately ten times larger than Peru's second city, Arequipa, and Buenos Aires ten times larger than Córdoba. Certainly, Latin America tends to contain more primate cities than most other parts of the world. Among the twenty Latin American republics only Bolivia, Brazil, Colombia, Ecuador, and Honduras do not have a primate city whose population exceeds that of the second city of the country by at least three times. Even among the exceptions, Brazil, Ecuador and Honduras hardly count since they contain two cities both of which greatly exceed the population of the third city in the country.

Urban primacy has long been present in Latin America. It was certainly encouraged by the political and administrative centralism instituted by Portuguese and Spanish rule and which was accentuated after

Figure 2.2
Latin America's giant cities, 1990

Table 2.4
Latin America's giant cities, 1990

CITY	Population (millions)
MEXICO CITY	20.19
SAO PAULO	17.40
BUENOS AIRES	11.51
RIO DE JANEIRO	10.71
LIMA	6.25
BOGOTA	4.85
SANTIAGO (CHILE)	4.73
CARACAS	4.10
BELO HORIZONTE	3.60
GUADALAJARA	3.16
PORTO ALEGRE	3.12
MONTERREY	2.97
RECIFE	2.49
SALVADOR	2.40
BRASILIA	2.36
SANTO DOMINGO	2.20
HAVANA	2.10
FORTALEZA	2.09
CURITIBA	2.03

Source: United Nations, Department of International Economic and Social Affairs, (1991)
Note: Some of the figures are clearly over-estimates, e.g. Caracas, Mexico City and São Paulo, but for the sake of consistency have not been corrected.

independence. It was encouraged further by the port locations of most of the capital cities, an advantage which allowed them to control the flows of most exports and imports. During the twentieth century, the strategy of encouraging industrial development behind high tariff walls and the active involvement of government in the process increased the advantages of the capital cities. As a result, most Latin American countries developed urban systems which became increasingly distorted. As an example, Santiago had 1.3 times as many people as Valparaíso in 1875, 2.8 times as many in 1920, and 7 times as many in 1971. Lima was 8 times larger than Arequipa in 1940 but 11 times larger in 1972.

Notes

(1) There are, of course, major exceptions, such as most of the cities in the Amazon area including such famous new cities as Brasília and Ciudad Guayana, Venezuela, yet such exceptions are surprisingly few in number.

(2) Until the eighteenth century, most of the Spanish realm in North and Central America was administered as part of the Viceroyalty of Spain and most of South America (plus Panama) as part of the Viceroyalty of Peru.

(3) The outbreak of cholera in Lima which was first announced in January 1991 was untypical by modern Latin American standards.

(4) An argument put forward by many social scientists in the 1950s when they realised how rapidly Latin American cities were growing and when they saw that the process of economic development was different in important respects from that in the developed countries.

Further reading

Good general introductions to Latin America's economic, social and historical background are given in Collier *et al.* (1985), Cubitt (1987), and Green (1991). Good accounts of the historical dimension of Latin American urbanisation are given by Hardoy (1975), Morse (1971), Newson (1987) and Sargent (1993).

For discussions of population growth, see Blouet and Blouet (1982), Sánchez-Albornoz (1974) and Merrick (1986). For information on urban primacy, see Gilbert and Gugler (1992) and Skeldon (1990).

3

THE MOVE
TO THE CITY

Migration in Latin America is hardly new. Columbus only 'discovered' indigenous peoples in the Americas because of their earlier arrival from Asia, and movement from the countryside was common in Peru during the time of the Incas. Internal migration accelerated in colonial times, and became ever more frequent later. The only things that changed over time were the direction and size of the migration flows.

The first great flood of people to Latin America's cities began in the late nineteenth century. The migrants to Buenos Aires, Montevideo and São Paulo were different from later arrivals, however, insofar as few of the newcomers came from Latin America at all. The majority originated from the impoverished rural areas of Italy and Spain, while others came from Germany. The immigrants came to work in the booming economies of Argentina, Uruguay and southern Brazil, arriving in the large port cities, where most of them stayed. As a result, the urban population exploded. The number of inhabitants in Buenos Aires increased from 242,000 in 1869 to 813,000 in 1895 to 2.13 million in 1914. According to James Scobie (1974), in 1910, three out of four *porteños* had been born abroad.

After 1914, fewer foreigners moved to Latin America. Some Spanish and US migrants moved to Cuba, and some Lebanese families and European Jews sought a refuge in Latin America in the 1930s, but from around 1940, most cityward migrants came from Latin America itself. Henceforth, most international migration was either out of the region, mainly towards the United States, or involved movement from one Latin American country to another.

Such movements were dwarfed, however, by the numbers of people who moved from the countryside to the city. For thirty years, migration became the main source of urban growth. Latin America was on its way to becoming a predominantly urban region.

That rural inhabitants should eventually move to the cities is not

THE HISTORY OF MIGRATION IN THE MANTARO VALLEY OF HIGHLAND PERU

Migration affected the valley during the Inca period as the Inca state established colonies throughout the valley. The Inca state required the valley inhabitants to labour for short period of the year in the highland mines. With the Conquest came the immigration of Spanish settlers and the emigration of valley peasants to work in the mines. The Spanish settlers accumulated land and portions were also allocated to the Catholic Church. Thus, land was removed from the control of the indigenous community which occasionally disputed this appropriation. Valley dwellers were also required by the Spanish not only to work in the mines but also to render labour-services in the major municipal centres.

The late nineteenth and early twentieth centuries witnessed not only the passage of traders and colonists but also the increasing emigration of valley peasants to the nearby mines of Yauli, Morococha and Cerro de Pasco. To meet the labour demand in the mines, workers were recruited through the *enganche* system. *Enganche* was labour-contracting through debt. A labour-recruiter would forward a peasant a small sum of money and the peasant was then required to work off the debt by labouring in the mines.

However, the danger of the work and the high accident rate meant that in time, coercion was more frequently used. When a miner fell ill or died without completing his contract, he left outstanding a debt which could be paid off either by one of his family - his son, for example - working off the requisite number of days, or by his family raising the cash - for instance, by selling land.

For most of the twentieth century, migration patterns from the village of Ataura have been dominated by the mining sector, and by the Cerro de Pasco Corporation. By the second decade of the twentieth century, *ataurinos* had gained *empleado* (employeee) positions in the Corporation. *Empleados* from Ataura would then recruit other *ataurinos* and thus village networks expanded throughout the Corporation. Several *ataurinos* became *empleados* in the refinery which the Corporation built in La Oroya, some eighty kilometres from the valley. The rapid outflow of men to the mining sector left a village of women, children and aged.

However, the Depression of the 1930s resulted in men moving back into the agricultural sector, and the migrant wage labourers of Ataura became poor peasants once more on their own plots of land. For many, however, the 1930s was a period marked by endless journeys seeking work.

With the boom of the 1940s, there was a shift away from mining, characterised by its low, fixed wage-rate, into occupations in Lima. The *ataurinos* could earn a living either in construction work or in the informal, self-employed, sector washing cars of selling newspapers, for in these occupations no capital was required.

> Working away from the village for ten years or more is now the pattern for most *ataurinos*, although in this general pattern there remain the frequent returns to the village due to brief pauses between jobs.
> **Source:** Laite (1984)

surprising since some had long been used to moving seasonally to seek agricultural work. Harvesting and sowing was often performed by migrant workers; the northeast of Brazil has a long tradition of mobile rural labour. Many rural workers had already been moving to the cities on a temporary basis, either because they had been compelled to do so or in order to supplement their meagre incomes. After 1930, however, cityward migration tended to become permanent. Although some migrants returned to the countryside because they had made money, and others because they had not, by far the greater number stayed in the cities.

The rural scene

Over the years, people have moved from the countryside to the towns because urban living conditions were superior. Recent figures on poverty in urban and rural areas show clearly that city-dwellers live better than most rural communities. The United Nations calculated in 1986 that whereas 36 per cent of city-dwellers lived in poverty, 60 per cent of rural Latin Americans were poor. As Pfeffermann and Griffin (1989:4-5) put it: "No matter how poverty is measured, the most common characteristic of the poor in Latin America is rural residence." In the case of Brazil, "in 1985, roughly 18 per cent of all people lived in households with per capita incomes below a fourth of the minimum wage. Of this group, 58 per cent were rural, although only 27 per cent of the total population lived in rural areas."

Similar findings emerge from recent surveys of poverty in several Latin American countries. Using two criteria of poverty, the proportion of the population living below a given level of income and the proportion of people who lack the basic ingredients for a decent quality of life, the United Nations calculate that rural households in Colombia and Peru are three times as likely as urban households to be poor (Table 3.1). In Peru, three out of four country-dwellers were classified as being desperately poor, compared to less than one-quarter of urban inhabitants. In Peru, nineteen out of twenty country-dwellers are thought to be poor and in Colombia almost four rural households out of five.

Other kinds of social indicator show a similar picture. Infant mortality, for example, is much higher in rural areas: 79 babies died in rural Mexico per thousand live births compared to 29 urban babies; in Peru, the figures were 101 and 54 respectively. Perhaps more surprising is that malnutrition

Table 3.1
Rural and urban poverty in Colombia and Peru
(% of households)

COUNTRY	DEGREE OF POVERTY	RURAL	URBAN	TOTAL
PERU 1985-6	Basic needs and low income	74.6	22.7	40.7
	Basic needs or low income	95.8	57.4	70.7
COLOMBIA 1988	Basic needs and low income	40.8	14.6	25.7
	Basic needs or low income	77.9	50.2	62.0

Source: Fresneda *at al.* (1991:33 and 55)

has long been more common in the countryside. In the late 1970s, for example, 62 per cent of rural families in the region were malnourished compared to 26 per cent of urban families. Clearly, some families suffer as farmers are forced to sell food to pay off their debts, and few landless rural households can afford to buy much food, especially during periods of unemployment.

Housing conditions are also worse in the rural areas. In Colombia, every room in the countryside in 1981 contained an average of 2.3 persons compared to only 1.6 persons in urban homes. The differential is still worse when measured in terms of services. Only 35 per cent of rural households in Colombia have electricity compared to 97 per cent of urban homes. Access to safe water is also a major problem in the rural areas.

Why are living standards so low in the countryside? One answer is that rural wealth has long been distributed in an extremely unequal way. Land has been concentrated in the hands of the few ever since the Spanish and Portuguese invaded in the sixteenth century. Even where serious efforts at land reform have been attempted, the distribution of land has rarely improved for long. As a result, few rural families have enough land to maintain a decent standard of living and many have no land at all. The shortage of land has certainly worsened as mortality rates in the countryside have fallen and the size of the average family has increased. Smaller plots require more intensive cultivation, but poverty hinders efforts to raise productivity. Poor farmers can seldom afford fertiliser or better seeds, and

Poor peasant housing in Peru Gabino Quispecondori/Ayaviri/TAFOS

raising yields by applying more labour to the land has its limits. The only real alternatives for the poor are to work on other people's land and to find other kinds of employment with which to supplement their income. As we shall see, migration sometimes plays a significant role in attempts to raise rural incomes.

Although agrarian reform programmes have been enacted in many Latin American countries, few have had much effect. Radical programmes were introduced in Bolivia, Chile, Cuba, Guatemala, Mexico, Nicaragua and Peru but subsequent governments returned most of the expropriated land in Chile, Guatemala and Peru, and time has gradually undermined the beneficial effects of the reform in Bolivia and Mexico. In recent years, the commercialisation of farming has sometimes worsened inequality. In Brazil, a vast increase in the area devoted to sugar-cane for gasahol petrol substitution has led to large numbers of small farmers being displaced from the land. In addition, a substantial increase in agricultural exports has been achieved through the introduction of more capital-intensive forms of production. The substitution of black beans by soya, for example, has led to the eviction of many tenant farmers. In Mexico, the growing involvement of transnational capital has transformed parts of the countryside, displacing many small farmers, even if it may simultaneously have increased the demand for temporary farm labour.

Rural livelihoods have also been hurt by the falling prices paid for most foodstuffs. Over the years, many governments have responded to political demands for cheaper food and have reduced the prices paid to small farmers for basic staples. While rich farmers have often gained compensation through higher subsidies, the weak have received little help. During the long phase of import-substituting industrialisation, the terms of trade turned against agricultural producers.

Increases in population have aggravated all of these problems. Family planning is not widely practised in the countryside, and falling rates of mortality have led to substantial increases in family size. Faster out-migration has been the only way in which rural households could cope. By the 1970s, the outflow was such that the rural population in many countries actually began to decline.

If rural poverty has been the main cause of out-migration, the flow in particular areas has been further accentuated by natural disasters and political violence. Floods, drought and hurricanes have brought grave problems for certain rural districts. Terrible droughts have frequently affected the northeast of Brazil, a region where three out of five poor Brazilians live. The Caribbean coast of Central America has been hit regularly by hurricanes. Elsewhere, earthquakes, lava flows, floods and frost have forced thousands of families to leave the land.

Political violence has sometimes increased the rural exodus. Since 1980, hundreds of thousands of families have been affected by the civil war in Nicaragua and by violence in Colombia, El Salvador, Guatemala and Peru. The brutal tactics of the Shining Path guerrillas and the equally violent response of the Peruvian military have caused thousands to flee to the cities. The combined impact of the drug barons, the guerrillas and the military in several regions of Colombia has had a similar effect. Recently, too, official efforts to destroy the coca crop in Bolivia, Colombia, Ecuador and Peru, in a forlorn attempt to reduce the flow of cocaine into the US, have caused widespread distress for a peasantry which has cultivated coca for thousands of years. Programmes to replace the lost income with substitute crops have simply proved inadequate.

The nature of migration

It is not rural poverty so much as the difference between urban and rural living standards that is the essential cause of most cityward migration. While people living in areas of violence or in regions subject to natural disasters may move to save their lives, poverty rarely pushes people off the land. As Merilee Grindle (1988:43) observes for Mexico: "The data suggest that sender households are not generally among the poorest of rural dwellers, nor are they among the most well-to-do." If lack of land, starvation, or poverty were the principal factors behind out-migration, then the figures should show a relatively higher proportion of poor migrants in the total flow. The

Table 3.2
Some characteristics of migrants to Bogotá, Mexico City and Valencia

	BOGOTA	MEXICO CITY	VALENCIA
Mean age on arrival (years)	29	25	29
% migrants who had worked previously in agriculture	62	70	30
Migrated:			
Alone	37	29	27
With spouse/children	43	28	48
With parents or kin	15	40	16
% receiving assistance on arrival	52	66	52
Schooling:			
None	19	28	35
Incomplete primary	37	41	26
Complete primary	31	22	28
At least some primary	13	12	11

Source: Gilbert and Ward (1986:35)

fact that they do not suggests that ,however difficult rural conditions, there is an important component in migration flows that can only be explained in terms of choice. The people who move are those who under current conditions can best adapt to the city. They make a rational choice between alternatives. Of course, what they are offered in the city may not represent much improvement, but it is some kind of choice nonetheless. As Julian Laite (1984:124-5) concludes with reference to Peru:

This is not the massive alienation of poor peasants from the land. In fact, the range of people who migrate and the range of reasons why they do so are more striking features. As well as the poor peasants looking for work to make subsistence possible, there are the subsistence peasants themselves, seeking savings to purchase tools, animals or even land, or looking for training possibilities either in trade or in further education.

Insofar as it is possible to generalise, most migrants move for economic reasons. But, while most migrants are looking to improve their lives, migration is often highly selective. Most surveys show that certain groups move more frequently: young adults, particularly women, the better educated and those with skills. Table 3.2 provides a summary of some of the main characteristics of adult migrants interviewed in the self-help settlements of Bogotá, Mexico City and Valencia (Venezuela) in 1978 and 1979. While this sample is unrepresentative of every kind of migrant, for it clearly excludes most rich and middle-class families, it does bring out several distinctive features of the migration process.

The first feature of interest is that most of the migrants in the sample were young. Even though migrants under 16 years were excluded, the mean age on arrival was still between 25 and 29 years. Second, while many migrants had previously worked in agriculture, one-third of the migrants to Bogotá and Mexico City sample and two-thirds of those to Valencia had had some other kind of job. Third, the migrants moved to the city at different stages in their life-cycle; some moved alone, some came with their spouse and children, some with their parents. Fourth, many received assistance on arrival in the city, substantially easing their adjustment to urban life (see below). Finally, few of the migrants had no education, and the majority could certainly read and write.

Surveys generally show that education is a key factor in the migration process. Migrants are almost always more educated than those who stay in the countryside. Some, indeed, have moved to the city to further their education because there are few secondary schools in the rural areas. Those who move also tend to be young (most are between 15 and 40 years of age), whereas those who stay in the countryside are much older. The out-migration of the young is something that now accentuates rural problems; the villages now contain a high proportion of old people.

Another significant aspect of Latin America's migration flow is that women are more likely to move than men. Table 3.3 shows that there are more females than males in most large Latin American cities.[1] In San José, there are only 88 men to every 100 women and in Bogotá and Santiago only 91. The disparity becomes much more obvious within the age groups which are most likely to contain migrants. Among the 20-24 year age group in Bogotá, for example, there were only 81 men for every 100 women in 1985. In Guadalajara, William Winnie's 1987 data on the characteristics of migrants reveal that only 82 men moved to the city between 1975 and 1984 for every 100 women.

Table 3.3
Sex ratios in selected cities

CITY	YEAR	MALES PER HUNDRED WOMEN
BOGOTA, COLOMBIA	1985	91
CARACAS, VENEZUELA	1990	92
GUADALAJARA, MEXICO	1986	97
MARACAIBO, VENEZUELA	1990	93
SAN JOSE, COSTA RICA	1984	88
SANTIAGO, CHILE	1992	91
VALPARAISO, CHILE	1992	93

Source: National population censuses and Chant (1992)

Of course, men move in much greater numbers to mining towns and to major new industrial cities where most of the available work is only open to men. But women dominate the flows to most large cities where there are plenty of jobs waiting for them, in domestic service, office cleaning, shop work, street selling and, sadly, prostitution. The large number of women working as domestic servants in middle-class homes is a significant feature of the job market and young women are often recruited directly from the countryside. The case of a Peruvian woman, Carmen, described by William Mangin (1970a:49), is not unusual: "Carmen had come to Lima at the age of fourteen from the southern highland province of Ayacucho. She had been sent by her mother and stepfather to work as a servant in the house of a Lima dentist, who was also a landowner in Ayacucho". But the initial experience of city life is not always a positive one, as Carmen's story shows:

> The dentist promised to 'educate' her but, in fact, she was not only not allowed to go to school but was rarely allowed outside the house. During her third year with the dentist's family her mother, who had left her stepfather in Ayacucho, rescued her from the dentist's house after a terrible row. Her mother then found a maid's job for Carmen where she was paid.

To which cities do migrants move?

The rapid growth of the major metropolitan areas means that large numbers of migrants have moved directly to the largest cities. However, many have

Figure 3.1
Origin of migrants to Guadalajara: 1975-1984

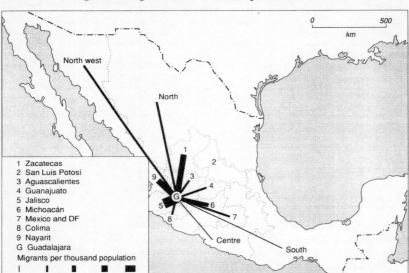

Source: Winnie (1987)

moved to smaller cities as well. Indeed, if the growth rates of larger and smaller cities in the 1950s, 1960s and 1970s are compared, it is clear that the population of many small cities increased far more quickly than those of the giants. In Peru, Chimbote's population grew 35 times between 1940 and 1972 due to the construction of a new steelworks and to a boom in the fishmeal industry. In Venezuela, the number of inhabitants in the new city of Ciudad Guayana grew almost five fold between 1950 and 1961 and more than doubled in the following decade. In Brazil, many towns in the Amazon region grew very rapidly, the urban population of Rondonia increasing 3.8 fold during the 1970s. And, in Mexico, the border town of Tijuana doubled in size in the 1960s. In one important sense, therefore, migrants are not fussy and will move wherever there is work. If governments choose to stimulate economic activity in the middle of nowhere, then migrants will move there; after all, both Brasília and Ciudad Guayana grew to be major cities in a couple of decades.

Those bound for the city are quite prepared to travel long distances, even if the majority of migrants make only a short journey. Why move a long way if refuge, employment opportunities or a better life can be found nearby? Figure 3.1 shows how the majority of migrants to Guadalajara have moved relatively short distances. While significant numbers have come from Mexico City, Monterrey and other major cities, the bulk of the migrants have come from the nearby states of Jalisco, Michoacán and Zacatecas.

Changes in the migration process

During the 1930s and 1940s, and in the poorer countries until much later, migration was not all that easy. Transportation was poor and it took a long time to reach the city, or for that matter to move to temporary work in the countryside. Gradually, migration began to cover much greater distances, and research in Peru shows how migrants, who once moved locally, increasingly moved to the major cities. Ronald Skeldon (1990:71-2) attempts to generalise this experience, arguing that:

> The mobility field of a group of individuals evolves from one based on short-term moves within a local ambit through stages of greater complexity when the field extends, with migrants spending longer at destinations and tending to move several times to several destinations, to one of greater simplicity based on direct moves for a long duration (ultimately permanent) to a single destination which, in this case, was the national capital.

Perhaps the most important difference between the 1930s and the present day is that migration in the 1930s was almost an adventure. Those who undertook it had little in the way of guidance. They might be told about work in some distant place, but they did not know what conditions were like there and most importantly they had no personal contacts. Therefore, it tended to be the adventurous, perhaps only the reckless, who migrated. Some only moved because they were hooked by labour contractors, when drunk, to sign contracts to work in unknown places.

Gradually, however, migrating became easier. Roads improved, there were more buses and the cost of travelling fell. In addition, former migrants, now established in the cities, offered beachheads for new arrivals. Former migrants would find their sisters jobs in domestic service, factory work for their brothers. Established migrants could also provide shelter for the newcomers, especially when owner-occupation in self-help settlements became increasingly common. As the difficulty of finding work and accommodation was eased and as transportation became quicker and cheaper, it is not surprising that more people began to move to the cities. There was less risk involved with family and friends already in the city. In any case, it was very much easier to get home if things did not work out.

Over time, these changes had an effect on the kind of people who moved. While we do not know for certain, it is likely that the process has gradually become less selective. It is now much easier for both the young and the old to avoid the kinds of danger that were inherent in earlier periods of migration. According to Merilee Grindle (1988: 44): "migratory networks have developed that channel migration from particular households and particular communities to particular destinations, cushion the entry into the labor market of new migrants, and provide social support for the migrants and their families in the sending community."

Not only has migration become easier because of the growing links between town and country, it has also become normal behaviour. Analysing the situation in highland Peru, Julian Laite (1984:124-5) reports: "When asked, the respondents themselves observed that nowadays everyone migrates, whether he be rich or poor. The rich look for professional work not to be found in the village, whilst the poor complement their rural interests with migration." It may even have become so easy that the extent of migration is now a problem. For Grindle (1988:47), "perhaps the most disturbing aspect of the migration process for the local community is the fact that it seems to feed upon itself: labor migration stimulates dependence on migratory income and thus requires further migration." Whether or not extensive migration has become 'disturbing' is highly debateable, but it has clearly become part of the survival strategy of many rural households.

Many studies emphasise how important remittances from migrants are in allowing rural families to survive. Individual migrants send part of their income to the family back home and regional associations mobilise funds to help pay for the installation of electricity or for a new school building back 'home'. Such regional associations have not only eased the process of migration into the city but have reciprocated by channelling funds back to the village. Today, and perhaps for some time, "off-farm employment cannot be considered a residual source of income for rural households; for many, it is their principal means for meeting their economic needs" (Grindle, 1988:171).

If migration has increased in volume as a result of economic change, better communications have made a permanent move less necessary. In a real sense, better transport has enlarged the urban area. People can now live in places quite far from the city and yet earn their living from the urban market. Small-scale manufacturers, traders and others can live in small towns fifty miles or more from the city but sell their produce there. Either they can get to the city or wholesalers can reach them. Better transportation has brought urbanisation of the countryside. A kind of *in-situ* migration has been taking place; a permanent move is unnecessary because the city has absorbed the country.

Better transport has also changed the way in which people migrate.

In nineteenth-century Britain, migrants moved to the cities in a series of steps. A similar step pattern used also to be true of Latin America, something that was welcomed by many sociologists because it was supposed to help accustom the migrants to urban life before they arrived in very large cities. It seems, however, that step migration has become less common. Indeed, what is the point now that most large cities can be reached in a single day's travel? As Ronald Skeldon (1990: 71) points out: "the large-scale surveys of migration to Lima and Cuzco in the 1960s showed that 78.8 and 65.1 per cent respectively had migrated in a single move from their place of birth to their destination."

The process of migration has clearly changed through time as the wider economic and social environment has changed. Better transportation, growing rural populations, more jobs in the cities, and a greater awareness of the opportunities available in the cities are bound to have affected the kinds of people who move, their destinations and their motives. These interrelationships between migration and socio-economic change have become even more obvious since 1980 when severe economic problems began to hit most of Latin America's cities.

The impact of economic recession

The debt crisis severely reduced the chances of getting a job in the urban areas. As we shall see in the next chapter, rates of unemployment increased as factories closed, governments laid off staff and consumer spending fell. Even for those in work, conditions deteriorated as wage rates plummeted. For the first time in at least three decades, many urban areas felt the full impact of recession. Of course, the effect varied from city to city. The removal of import tariffs and customs duties clearly hit employment in cities heavily reliant on industrial activity. In Mexico, several of Monterrey's major factories closed, and Gustavo Garza (1991) claims that in Mexico City, 250,000 industrial jobs were lost as 6,000 companies closed their doors. By contrast, Mexico's border cities flourished on the basis of export production.

Some parts of the Latin American countryside also fared relatively well. More competitive exchange rates allowed new agricultural products to be sold abroad. Timber, fruit, fish and vegetables began to be exported in increasing quantities. In places, the traditional gulf in living standards between city and country began to narrow. If incomes were improving on the farms and jobs were no longer available in the cities, there was much less reason to migrate to the city.

Not only did worsening conditions in the city discourage newcomers, they even forced some city-dwellers to move out. While there is still a shortage of adequate data, urbanisation certainly slowed and in places migration clearly stopped.[2] Local academics suspect that as many people moved out of Santiago in the 1970s and 1980s as moved in. The rate of migration to Mexico City also slowed dramatically as the city's population grew by possibly as little as 1.4 per cent during the 1980s.

The recession increased the interdependence of the rural and urban branches of a family and may have encouraged movement in both directions. Flows of migrants to the city no doubt continued, but some city dwellers became more dependent on their kin in the countryside. Food produced on the family farm became a vital supplement to the urban diet.

The effects of migration on the city

When migration became common in the 1940s and 1950s, the urban authorities became very anxious about the arrival of such large numbers of ill-educated rural people. Would migrants with few skills be able to cope with the demands of urban life? Could sufficient jobs be created to provide them with work? Could they be adequately housed? If the answer to these questions was no, would migration eventually lead to political unrest?

The academic literature of the time certainly reflected these attitudes. Consider, for example, the summary made by Daniel Lerner as late as 1967:

> The point that must be stressed in referring to this suffering mass of humanity displaced from the rural areas to the filthy peripheries of the great cities is that few of them experience the 'transition' from agricultural to urban-industrial labour called for by the mechanism of development and the model of modernization. They are neither housed, nor trained, nor employed nor serviced. They languish on the urban periphery without entering into any productive relationship with its industrial operations. They are the 'displaced persons' of the developmental process as it now typically occurs in most of the world, a human flotsam and jetsam that has been displaced from traditional agricultural life without being incorporated into modern industrial life (Lerner, 1967:24-5).

It must already be clear to the reader that these fears were unjustified. The migrants were not the flotsam and jetsam Lerner described. Many could read and write, and most had skills of use in the urban environment. Most important of all, the migrants were adaptable. People from indigenous areas quickly learned to speak Spanish. On arrival, most changed their dress in an effort to hide their humble origins, shedding the practical poncho that town people associated with rusticity. Migrants changed their ways because there was no real alternative; the city dwellers made fun of their customs and values.

FROM 'INDIAN' VILLAGE TO 'MEXICAN' CITY: THE ADAPTABILITY OF THE CITYWARD MIGRANT

In the early 1960s Douglas Butterworth studied the lives of Mixtec Indians who had migrated to Mexico City from Tilantongo in the State of Oaxaca. The following excerpts from Butterworth (1962) illustrate both the reasons why migrants leave the countryside and how successfully most migrants adapt to the city.

"The main motivations for migration to urban centres are economic and educational, the family heads are unanimously agreed that they are better off financially in Mexico City than in Tilantongo. Almost all informants own radios. Two families have television sets. Sanitation is greatly improved over that in Tilantongo; an outdoor privy is owned individually or shared by a number of families.

The diet of migrants is without exception much improved. Food is generally cited as the material evidence of the improved standard of living. Whereas in Tilantongo the normal diet is limited to tortillas and salt, beans being eaten only one or twice a week and meat weekly or semi-monthly, in Mexico City beans are eaten daily and meat is eaten at least once a week by even the poorest families. The better-off families in the city eat meat daily.

The only forms of entertainment in Tilantongo, where there is no electricity, are drinking, gossip, the annual fiestas, and, for the young men, basketball. In the city, drinking and visiting are combined with watching TV or listening to the radio. The migrants do not go to the movies, nor to so-called 'cultural' activities, such as art galleries.

A universal change is a remarkable reduction in the importance of religion. All claim to be sincere believers, however, none of the thirty-one family heads goes to church, except for ceremonies such as baptism and confirmation.

Changes in dress are part of the de-Indianization process undergone by migrants. Typical garb in Tilantongo is a white cotton shirt and white trousers worn by the men and a cotton dress and a head-shawl by the women. All men wear sandals; most women go barefoot. All the men wear hats woven from palm leaves. In Mexico City, many of the women change their attire, retaining the cotton dress, but replacing the shawl with a sweater. The men discard all 'Indian' dress that they wore in their village. Ties are worn for special events. Each man owns either a suit or a sports jacket. Shoes are worn by all men; the straw hat has been discarded.

The explanation for the successful adaptation to city life by Tilantongo migrants probably lies in a well-balanced combination of maintenance of strong emotional ties within the family, with fellow migrants from Tilantongo, and with their *tierra*, and a plastic ability to learn new skills and values."

Family links were vital in the process of adjustment. The presence of an older brother, uncle or aunt in the city was a critical factor in finding a job and shelter and, generally, in establishing contacts. But so, too, were the so-called voluntary associations which emerged in many cities but whose activities have been most extensively documented in Lima. While there is some dispute over the value of such associations to migrants and over why such associations developed more prolifically in some cities than in others, they clearly provided friendship networks which helped the new arrivals. At the very least, they helped entertain the newcomers, offering them leisure activities and introducing them to new friends.

Such was the adaptability of the migrants that they quickly merged into the urban landscape. The worst fears of the authorities were unfounded. They did not cause riots or even protest, since they felt better off in the city than in the countryside. And, having established themselves as best they could, the last thing they wanted to do was cause trouble. The newcomers' greatest wish was to be inconspicuous and as a result they were usually politically conservative (see Chapter Seven).

If migrants did much better than was expected, that did not mean that they lived well. Although most improved their living standards, they still lived in desperately poor housing and earned very little. They might not have been radical, subversive or wished to stand out from the crowd but those characteristics should not be interpreted to mean that all was well. As William Mangin pointed out in 1970:

> The early stereotype held by most middle and upper class Peruvians of the *barriada* dwellers as illiterate, nonproductive, lawless, recent communistic Indian migrants is still held by many - but is giving way among young architects, politicians, academics, and anthropologists to an equally false picture. Perhaps as an antidote to the first, it paints them as happy, contented, literate, productive, adjusted, politically conservative-forever, patriotic citizens. They are, in fact, about like the vast majority of Peruvians, moderately to desperately poor, cynical and trusting of politicians, bishops, outside agitators, and their own local leaders. They are alternatively hopeful and despairing about the future of their children and themselves.

Return migration

While we lack a great deal of information on return migration, the move back home is certainly not uncommon. Some migrants return because their families need their help in the countryside. Sarah Radcliffe (1992:42) describes the case of Luisa who was working as a servant in Cuzco.

Although she had originally anticipated being away for a long period, she went back to the village after four months when her father fell ill (her mother required assistance), but then travelled to Puerto Maldonado as a cook for the gold-panning workers. During this time, her father died and Luisa returned definitively to Kallarayan, as her mother needed help with the animals and fields.

Other migrants may return because they are unhappy with urban life: those who cannot get work and those who dislike the city. However, in one survey in northern Mexico, Jorge Balán *et al.* (1973:166) concluded that few of those who returned to their village from Monterrey were forced out of the city. Many returned for family reasons but others returned because they had been successful. Clearly, some migrants manage to accumulate capital during their urban sojourn. They may decide to open a shop, build a nice house, or buy land in their home village, perhaps the main motive behind the original move.

Still others maintain a peripatetic life-style, moving constantly between city and country. Indeed, some writers argue that so many people now float between the two worlds that the distinction between town and country has effectively broken down. Norman Long and Bryan Roberts (1984:161), for example, claim that:

Much of the contemporary population of Huancayo (in Central Peru) is clearly a floating population. Many traders keep a room in Huancayo for use for some days in the month, but may keep their families elsewhere - in their home village, for example. The city is still, to a certain extent, a temporary dormitory for some of its working population, in which the man sleeps during the week but returns to the village and his family at weekends. However, the increase in transport facilities permits many of these workers to live permanently in the nearby villages.

Later in the same book, the authors make a similar assessment about Lima: "This is a city made up, to a very large extent, of a floating population in which large in-flows of migrants are partly compensated by out-flows of returning migrants or of Lima-born people seeking work elsewhere." While my own experience in other parts of Latin America suggests that this is much less the case in other large cities, the extensive links between town and country are certainly not to be ignored.

Notes
(1) This method of calculation actually underestimates the true preponder-ance of women in migration flows, since most young people are born in the city (and up to the age of 15, boys outnumber girls) and because most cities contain relatively few old people (where women heavily outnumber men).

(2) See CED (1990) and Buchhofer and Aguilar (1991).

Further reading
Relevant information on patterns of migration can be found in Balán *et al.* (1973), Butterworth and Chance (1981: ch.3), Gilbert (1974: ch.4), Gilbert and Ward (1986), Merrick (1986) and Skeldon (1990).

For discussions of the effects of land reform, see Grindle (1988), and Townsend (1987) . The effects of agribusiness and agricultural commer-cialisation are discussed by Burbach and Flynn (1980), Sanderson (1985) and Goodman and Redclift (1981).

For the effects of violence on migration in Colombia, see Pearce (1990), and in Peru, see Palmer (1992).

For discussions of the role of gender in migration, see Chant (1992) and Gilbert and Gugler (1992:ch.3).

Interesting discussions on the role of remittances in sustaining rural life include Cornelius (1991) and Grindle (1989) on Mexico, and Doughty (1970), Jongkind (1974) and Long and Roberts (1984) on Peru.

For discussions of how migrants adapted to the 'alien' urban environment, see Butterworth (1962), Butterworth and Chance (1981), Mangin (1970) and Perlman (1976).

For discussion of the nature of 'marginality', see Perlman (1976) and Portes (1972).

Return migration to the countryside is discussed by Balán *et al.* (1973), Butterworth and Chance (1981), Long and Roberts (1984) and Skeldon (1990).

4

THE WORLD OF WORK

How do people earn a living?

The picture of thousands of bootblacks, street sellers and beggars thronging the streets dominates most people's view of the Latin American city. This negative image is compounded by the idea that the rest of the labour force is scraping a living by picking rubbish off garbage tips, slaving away in small workshops or working as domestic servants. Unfortunately, this stereotype has a great deal of validity. Large numbers of people do eke out a precarious living from one or other of these kinds of activity. Unfortunately, too, their numbers have increased in recent years, an inevitable consequence of the recession of the 1980s.

At the same time, it is important to remember that the majority of Latin American workers are not employed in these kinds of activities. Many, indeed, are working in much more 'formal' and 'respectable' activities. This fact is demonstrated in Figure 4.1 which gives information on work by sector for Guadalajara, showing that a considerable proportion of the labour force is engaged in office or white-collar work. More generally, school teachers, office workers, government officials and many different kinds of profes- sional worker are extremely numerous in Latin American cities.

Indeed, one of the major changes in the Latin American city in the post-war period has been the emergence of the middle class. By 1970, between 25 and 38 per cent of the total populations of Argentina, Chile, Colombia, Uruguay and Venezuela could be considered middle-class, and in the major cities the proportions were higher. In Bogotá, 44 per cent of the labour force in 1977 worked in white-collar occupations; in Guadalajara the figure was 48 per cent in 1988, and in Caracas 44 per cent the same year.[1]

Table 4.1 shows that commerce and services are by far the greatest generators of employment, with typically from half to three-quarters of jobs generated by non-manufacturing activities. While there are cities where commerce and services are much less important, industry rarely contributes

Figure 4.1
Occupational structure of Guadalajara, 1988

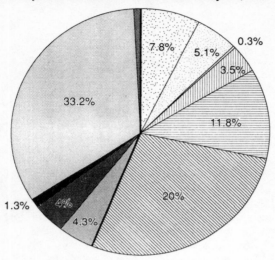

Blue collar

Domestic workers	
Transport workers	
Police, security and armed forces	
Industrial workers	
Other manual	

White collar

Professional and technical	
Education, art and entertainment	
Public administration	
Private managers and owners	
Office workers	
Sales staff	

more than 30 per cent of all jobs. And in most smaller cities (as the inclusion of Ciudad Bolívar, a small administrative and commercial city in Venezuela, shows), jobs in commerce and services dominate the employment structure.

Not only are large numbers of workers employed in commerce and services, but far too many people are engaged in activities that support a very low standard of living. This is a particularly severe problem in the poorer cities of the region. In cities such as La Paz, Cuzco or Lima, the majority are engaged in low-productivity work for which they receive little reward.

Table 4.1
Employment structures of selected cities

CITY	YEAR	INDUSTRY	COMMERCE AND SERVICES
CIUDAD GUAYANA	1986	29.7	55.3
CIUDAD BOLIVAR	1986	11.9	76.0
GUADALAJARA	1988	27.1	64.8
MONTERREY	1988	28.6	62.6
BOGOTA	1990	24.1	70.5

Source: DANE (1991); INEGI (1989); CVG (1987)

The theory of over-urbanisation

Concern has long been expressed about the numbers of people involved in low-paid work in Latin America's cities. Indeed, during the 1960s and 1970s, such concern crystallised into a particularly negative view of the role of urban services and their impact on social values and living standards. As the United Nations put it in 1973:

> The formation of a marginal and sub-marginal population, often living on the very edge of subsistence levels, was the most obvious price that the major Latin American towns had to pay for reconciling their high rates of population growth with the low levels of productivity of their economic structure. The barriadas, slums, shanty towns, favelas and so forth, which during the period 1945-60 spread and multiplied within the bounds of the urban horizon, must be regarded as indicators of a more general phenomenon: a huge sector of the urban population was living in economically, socially, and politically marginal conditions (UNECLA, 1973:159).

This analysis identifies three problems. The first is that people are supposedly involved in the wrong kinds of economic activity; there are too many working in services and too few in manufacturing or modern kinds of service activity. This imbalance became known as the tertiarisation phenomenon. The second problem is that as a result of their inferior jobs they do not participate 'properly' in the working of the city, they are marginal to 'normal' forms of urban behaviour and activity - the so-called marginality syndrome. The final problem is that the cities are thought to be growing too quickly with the implication that something should be done to slow the flow of migrants into the city. This is the over-urbanisation hypothesis. According to Gino Germani (1973:32): "In all the presently developing countries the growth of the urban population has occurred in much greater measure than the growth of the labor force working in industry."

This process of tertiarisation was clearly manifest in the massive statistical computations made by sociologists such as Kingsley Davis and Hilda Hertz (1954) who compared employment structures in modern 'developed' cities with those in 'less-developed' countries. The figures showed that the latter contained a far higher proportion of people in service activities. Even more significant was that Latin American cities contained many more people in services than had been characteristic of most nineteenth-century British, French, German and US cities. Service jobs in Latin America were not found in productive activities, such as medicine or education, but were appearing in unproductive occupations such as scavenging, begging and prostitution. Germani argued that "..a considerable proportion of the working-age population residing in cities were not absorbed in services of 'modern' type and remained marginal or relatively marginal to to the modern forms of the economy." Tertiarisation meant that the city was not contributing to economic growth and development. Indeed, the eminent Chicago sociologist, Bert Hoselitz, wrote a famous article in 1957 describing the functions of cities in developed countries as 'generative' and those of Third World cities as being 'parasitic'.

Through lack of alternatives, the Latin American poor were forced into unsavoury kinds of work. Because of their poverty, they were forced into insanitary forms of housing, living in overcrowded conditions and lacking adequate services. Their children did not attend school. They lived on the streets and were gradually absorbed into what Oscar Lewis (1966) defined as a 'culture of poverty'. Social marginality was the inevitable result: "People in this situation not only do not perform activities appropriate to a modern tertiary sector, but their consumption and life styles (although not necessarily their aspirations) continue to be largely marginal with regard to modern society" (Germani, 1973:38).

For many social scientists the implications were clear. If productive work was lacking, the population should not be in the cities at all. They were there only because they had been forced into the towns by poverty in the countryside. This is a recurring message in Latin America. The urban authorities are constantly complaining that there are too many people

Old and new business in Mexico City   Ron Giling/PANOS Pictures

demanding work and services. Every so often, a new incumbent to office, or one petitioned sufficiently strongly, will attempt to take the 'necessary' action to remedy this evil. Recently, the government of Campo Grande, capital of the state of Mato Grosso do Sul, offered to pay the bus fares home of people willing to leave the city.

Unemployment

According to the tertiarisation hypothesis, so many people worked in these kinds of low-paid activity because there was too little proper work, an inevitable result of the imbalance between population growth and the expansion of jobs. For, if the number of jobs was increasing impressively in many Latin American cities, the number of people seeking work was expanding still more quickly. As Alejandro Portes and Laura Benton (1984: 593) point out: "Between 1950 and 1980, the total Latin American economically active population grew at an annual rate of 2.5 percent, but the urban labor force increased at a rate of 4.1 percent per year." It was not just that large numbers of migrants were arriving in the city, but that over the years young migrants were also having their children there. As those children grew up, they needed jobs.

The imbalance between the growth of jobs and the numbers of people looking for work, however, was seldom reflected in the level of open unemployment. Indeed, rates of unemployment in most Latin American cities during the 1960s and 1970s were remarkably low. In 1970, open unemployment in Buenos Aires was 4.9 per cent, in Lima 6.9 per cent, in Santiago 4.1 per cent, in Brazil's seven largest cities 6.5 per cent and in Mexico's largest three cities 7.0 per cent. Only in Panama City and in Colombia's largest four cities did unemployment reach double figures. By current standards, even in developed countries, these were not high figures.

Of course, we should remember that the method of measuring unemployment in some countries certainly underestimated the problem. In Mexico, for example, individuals working one hour or more during the previous week are considered to have been employed! In Latin America, unlike in most developed countries, those without work also gain nothing from registering as unemployed. Since there is no form of unemployment benefit, the poor are virtually forced to find work of some kind. In general, while adults in the poorest families in developed countries are unemployed, those in Latin America are much more likely to be earning a living, albeit at a penurious level. In general, the term 'working poor' is a more appropriate description of the impoverished in Latin America than the term 'unemployed'.

These low rates of open unemployment suggested that it was low pay rather than the lack of jobs that was the major problem in most Latin American cities. Those who were actually without work were not a problem because they had chosen to be unemployed. In general, they were better off and much more educated than the working poor and the so-called 'luxury unemployment thesis' emerged to explain this phenomenon. It was thought that: "(1) unemployment is concentrated mostly in urban areas; (2) a large proportion of the unemployed are young individuals; (3) the typical unemployed is relatively well-educated; and, (4) a large proportion of the unemployed is economically dependent on other family members" (Tenjo, 1990:735).

Why should the better educated experience higher levels of unemployment? Al Berry (1975) argued that this was simply the most rational response in the absence of an appropriate job. A recent graduate was unlikely to come from a poor family. Unlike the unemployed manual worker, therefore, the graduate was not liable to be forced to work on the rubbish dump. Having paid for the graduate's education, a little more suffering was a disappointment for the family, but not much more. Not only did the lack of compulsion mean that a graduate did not have to find work on the streets, it was also a sensible medium-term earnings strategy. If a university graduate in law or medicine could not get a job immediately, it would be inappropriate to resort to selling cigarettes on the street. Far more sensible was to spend the period of unemployment attempting to cultivate contacts in order to obtain work in the future. Participation in an electoral

Table 4.2
Urban unemployment
(percentage)

CITY	1978	1980	1982	1984	1986	1988
BUENOS AIRES	2.8	2.3	4.7	3.8	4.6	na
BOGOTA	6.7	6.8	6.7	11.6	12.4	9.2
MEDELLIN	12.4	15.7	14.8	15.2	14.7	11.9
MEXICO CITY	6.9	4.3	4.0	5.8	5.1	na
LIMA	8.0	7.1	6.6	8.9	5.4	7.9
MONTEVIDEO	10.1	7.4	11.9	14.0	10.7	9.2
SANTIAGO, CHILE	13.7	11.8	20.0	18.5	13.1	11.2

Source: Gilbert (1990a:78)

campaign in support of a powerful politician might produce a decent job should that politician be elected. In the medium term, earnings would be maximised despite the period out of work.

Since 1980, of course, unemployment levels have shot up. Table 4.3 shows that the level of urban unemployment doubled in several cities during the 1980s.

The problem of unemployment has been particularly serious in many cities which had earlier benefited from rapid industrial development. The economic recession, combined with the adoption of a more open-door policy towards manufactured imports, wrought havoc in many industrial cities. Gustavo Garza (1991) estimates, for instance, that in Mexico City manufacturing employment declined by 25 per cent between 1980 and 1988. Other industrial cities in Latin America also suffered badly; Monterrey and Medellín both lost large numbers of manufacturing jobs and suffered from much higher rates of unemployment than other cities in the same country.

What kind of people have lost their jobs? Notwithstanding the luxury unemployment thesis, it seems as if unemployment has impacted most strongly on the weak and particularly on women and children. In their analysis of Mexico, Rolando Cordera and Enrique González (1990:29) point out: "In 1986, the average unemployment rate in the country's sixteen principal urban areas was 4.3 percent (6.1 per cent for workers aged twelve to fourteen, 11.9 per cent for the 15-19 age group, and 7.4 percent for the

20-24 year age group). For women the figures tell an even sadder tale: 14.5 per cent unemployment for women aged 15-19 and 8.3 percent for the 20-24 year olds." Generalising across the region, John Humphrey (1992:16) concludes: "It seems a characteristic of recessions in Latin America that not only does unemployment rise disproportionately among adults, and household heads, but also that the less educated and unskilled are most affected." His own results from a survey in São Paulo show that "the unemployment rate for heads without any education at 8.6 per cent is more than twice as high as the rate for heads with some secondary education. The lowest rate of unemployment is found among those with the highest level of education." In Lima, one of the cities most deeply afflicted by the recession, the pattern is the same. Paul Glewwe and Gillette Hall (1992:26) remark that whereas "in 1985-86 the unemployed were often those who were financially able to be selective as to their type of employment, ... by 1990 the body of unemployed was largely composed of those in poorer deciles who simply could not find work." Perhaps, the recession has made Latin America more like the rest of the world, albeit in a wholly unwelcome way.

Table 4.3
Urban informal work and level of economic development

COUNTRY	INFORMAL WORKERS (% of urban labour force in 1980)	NATIONAL PER CAPITA INCOME (1980 US$)
VENEZUELA	20.8	3.377
ARGENTINA	23.0	3,010
MEXICO	35.8	2,498
URUGUAY	23.1	2,417
CHILE	27.1	2,314
BRAZIL	27.2	2,049
ECUADOR	52.8	1,415
COLOMBIA	34.4	1,259
PERU	40.5	1,190

Source: Wilkie and Perkal (1984) and UNECLAC (1987:184)

The informal sector

In the absence of a welfare state, it is clear that most poor families are forced to find some kind of work, even when that work is both arduous and badly paid. Many of these impoverished workers are found in the informal sector, a problematic term that became popular in the 1970s and which, despite its unclear meaning, is a popular shorthand which is still in wide use. Table 4.3 employs this concept and shows how the proportion of the workforce with jobs in the petty services and manufacturing of the informal sector tends to be highest in the poorest countries of the region. My reading of this table is that in very poor countries, households survive by attempting to put as many workers as possible into the labour force. We will return to this argument below.

But what is the informal sector? The International Labour Organisation's Regional Employment Programme in Latin America (PREALC) defined the informal sector as the sum of the self-employed, excluding professionals, unremunerated family workers, and domestics, with all wage workers being included in the formal sector. In practice, this produced a highly conservative estimate, for as Alejando Portes and Laura Benton (1984:607) argue:

> In Latin America, perhaps with the exception of Argentina and Uruguay, this assumption leads to a gross overestimate of formal employment since a large proportion of wage workers are actually hired by mini-enterprises that are legally exempted from or simply do not observe protective labor codes. ... Whenever unprotected wage labor is added to the definition of informal employment, the relative size of the latter increases to about half the urban labor force.

Portes and Benton propose that a more important characteristic of the informal sector is its lack of legal protection and social security cover. While there are good reasons for supporting this kind of definition, it is not without its own difficulties, for as Victor Tokman (1989:42) observes: "...it is confusing to define as informal all those activities which operate beyond the regulation of the state. Not all unregulated activity is informal. For example, according to this criterion one would have to view as informal even those large modern enterprises which evade taxes or do not comply with labour laws." Some very affluent drug traffickers would also be included, unless they happened to be in jail!

Clearly, defining a myriad of different kinds of jobs as the informal sector is dangerous because it can include rich with poor, regularly paid with casual labour, and criminal with non-criminal activity. Certainly, any failure to distinguish between casual workers, regular wage labourers and the self-employed is likely to lead to poor policy formulation. Lisa Peattie (1987:857) puts it most strongly when she argues that: "as a framework for considering problems of poverty, it doesn't work because it is factually incorrect and politically obfuscating."

The dangers of lumping different kinds of activity into a single category are illustrated by the debate about how easy it is for the unemployed to enter informal sector activities. If the sector is to mop up unemployment, then ease of entry is critical. But, recent evidence from São Paulo shows that "the unemployed do not find it easy to enter the informal sector, and in particular they do not find it easy to enter into self-employment" (Humphrey, 1992:29). Clearly, it is necessary to distinguish between different kinds of occupation. While it is easy to enter activities such as begging or boot-blacking, activities which Bruno Lautier (1990:282) calls the 'survival informal sector', it is much more difficult to get into those kinds of activities which require skills, capital, know-how or contacts. Anyone can start begging at the traffic lights, clean shoes outside their own house or sell home-made cakes from their front room. It is much more difficult to set up a more sophisticated business or to progress into better paid kinds of service activity.

Perhaps this can best be illustrated by looking at some of the controls that impede entry into seemingly the most menial of activities. Consider, for example, the future of an unemployed worker contemplating a temporary career in boot-blacking - one of the informal sector activities most frequently criticised as both demeaning and poorly paid. The capital costs of setting up in business are not high: some polish and brushes, a box to carry the tools of the trade and to act as the 'work-bench', and perhaps a chair for the customer to sit on. Little working capital is needed, nor is the skill factor very high.

The problems come when the worker contemplates where to ply his new trade.[2] He can probably work in his own neighbourhood without too many problems but the best pitches are likely to be elsewhere, in the centre of town, in tourist areas or, even better, inside an office block. But such prime sites are not available because existing bootblacks will already occupy them. Some cities also insist that bootblacks have licences, and the police will harass a new bootblack operating in the centre of town without such a licence. The principal barrier to the most remunerative kind of site, access to a regular clientele in an office block, is likely to be different. The difficulty is to get past the doorman, and increasingly the armed guard which most office blocks now employ. Such entry will require either a commission to the gate-keepers or a familial tie of some kind; no doubt most doormen will allow their relatives in, while keeping others out. Even then, entrance is still limited to those wearing a suit or a uniform of some kind, since scruffy bootblacks may not be permitted even when they are known to the doorman.

Similar kinds of barriers impede entry to all of the more remunerative kinds of informal sector activity. Licences are required by street traders and without them they are liable to harassment by the police. They may be harassed anyway, as in Cali, Colombia, where "complaints about police brutality and corruption are frequent, and some officials even run neigh-bourhood 'protection rackets' charging each trader a daily or weekly sum in return for a promise of free business operation" (Bromley, 1978:1164). Such activities are likely to be particularly commonplace in the more affluent parts of town.

Few newcomers can penetrate this world easily or quickly. It takes time to learn the rules and to find ways to live within the system. As such, it is probably best to think of many informal activities as careers in which people may progress gradually upwards, as with the bootblack who ends up selling lottery tickets or the street trader who opens her own shop. Unfortunately, the route upwards is full of dangers and few will progress. Most informal occupations have little independence, receive only limited rewards and few have much scope for accumulating capital. As Ray Bromley puts it: "Many street traders are little more than disenfranchised employees of larger enterprises. They work for relatively low and variable remunerations and carry most of the risk in unstable and sometimes illegal activities."

What is the role of the informal sector?

Most economists have always viewed the informal sector as a way of mopping up surplus labour. This is what Bruno Lautier (1990) calls the 'survival informal sector', what Aníbal Quijano (1974) called the 'marginal pole' and Clifford Geertz (1973) and Terry McGee (1976) called 'urban involution'. According to this view, it is the sector of last resort, whose function is merely to help sustain those whose labour is not required in the capitalist sectors of the economy. It performs no effective economic role and contributes nothing to the modernisation process. It exists because there is no social welfare system, people survive by subdividing work between themselves. Despite considerable criticism of this interpretation, there can be little doubt that some part of the informal sector continues to play this role, especially during periods of recession.

At the same time, the various activities of the informal sector play many additional roles. A very important function is to act in support of the modern capitalist sector. Research in the 1970s showed clearly how the early notion that low-paid workers operated independently from modern enterprise was very far from the truth. Instead of being autonomous, formal and informal activities were integrally linked. Indeed, researchers in São Paulo argued that the very survival of capitalist enterprise in Latin America

THE WORK OF THE GARBAGE PICKERS

The largest group of garbage pickers found in Cali are those who go to work each day on the municipal garbage dump, which is located by the banks of the River Cauca on the eastern edge of the city. Some 400 people spend their day clustering around each truck as it arrives, or wandering over the dump, in search of whatever saleable materials can be found. Working with sticks and sacks they collect a variety of wastes and later sort them at the side of the dump before selling them. A second major group are those who work in the streets of Cali in conjunction with the routes taken by the municipal garbage trucks. Once the garbage cans have been brought out of the houses, and in the few seconds before the truck arrives, these garbage pickers take out what they can. Each truck tends to collect an average of six people working in front of it as it moves along, and hence there at least 300 of these pickers in the city. Finally there are those who work with no relation to the garbage collection system at all. Some of those work in the city centre collecting paper from the numerous shops and offices. Others work with carts and collect a more narrow range of materials, often having to buy them. They generally collect bottles, newspapers and certain kinds of scrap metals - articles which would lose their value if thrown into the garbage - and they can be seen wandering through the richer residential neighbourhoods of the city, shouting as they go. The size of this group is the most difficult to estimate, but it would seem that their number is between 500 and 1,000.

The types of material that are recuperated by the garbage picker are varied. The largest volume consists of paper and cardboard in its infinite variety of forms. This is processed to make a number of products such as tissues, cardboard and asphalted cardboard roofing tiles. Metals are also important, particularly scrap iron and steel, but also copper, bronze, aluminium or lead. Most of these materials find their way to one of the foundries, or to Cali's steel works, on the north side of the city. Bottles are a third major recuperated product, and perhaps the biggest single customer is the state-owned liquor factory in Cali, but substantial proportions go to other drinks factories and to laboratories and cosmetics firms. Bone is taken from the garbage and is almost the only source of bone for one section of the animal food industry, since it is dry enough to be used in the ovens. Plastics are a fast growing market for the waste business... many small plastics firms in Cali and elsewhere rely upon this source of raw materials.

The overall development of garbage picking is intimately related in its economic organization to big industry, not only in Cali, but throughout the whole of Colombia. If the steel industry is in crisis so are the scrap iron collectors. If the demand for waste paper goes up so do prices, and in all probability the number of garbage pickers as well... The garbage picker may work hard, may have a shrewd eye for saleable materials, may search long for the right buyer; in short, he may be the near-perfect example of the enterprising individual. It will not get him far.

Source: Birkbeck (1979)

depended on the contributions made by informal workers. Francisco de Oliveira (1985) and others demonstrated how large industrial companies contracted out work to numerous small companies. Some textile companies would 'put out' cloth to sempstresses in the *favelas*, who would put together up-market clothes for sale in local boutiques. Work in Colombia showed how activities seemingly totally divorced from the modern sector contributed actively to its survival. Ray Bromley and Chris Birkbeck's study of recycling in Cali, for example, showed how waste paper and bottles ended back in the production line. Rather than the garbage pickers being surplus to the needs of the productive sector, their labour reduced the cost of inputs to the modern plants. Similarly, it became clear that the myriad of street sellers and small shops was very useful to large companies. What better for a company producing cigarettes or chewing gum than to have a labour force on virtually every road junction and pavement in the city? Not only is the sales force ubiquitous, it is also very cheap.

Subcontracting, which appears to have increased in importance over the years in many of the larger cities, has prospered because it costs large firms much less to employ workers outside a factory. According to Victoria Lawson (1992:7): "..subcontracting ensures a supply of various types of labour that would be unacceptable within the unionized parent firm. Specifically, the fluctuating, labour-intensive phases of production can be performed by cheap, unorganized, unskilled, off-premises workers at considerable wage, and extra-wage, savings to the parent firm. This practice is common throughout the assembly industries in Latin America."

Not only does subcontracting provide firms with a cheap labour force, but it also offers them greater flexibility in case of hard times. Labour legislation in Latin America frequently prevents businesses from firing workers without expensive compensation. Workers can be hired extra-legally within the main plant and frequently are. But it is often much safer for a firm to employ people outside the plant, particularly when the one-off products are destined for an unpredictable and relatively unstable market. This is particularly common in the clothing industry where firms employ large numbers of sempstresses working from home. If their product does not sell, the companies need not give out any more cloth. If they had employed the workers in a factory, discontinuation of the product line would have been much more expensive.

It has also been argued that the informal sector plays a further vital role in capital accumulation by cutting the cost of labour in modern factories. The first way it does this is by acting as an 'industrial reserve army' (Oliveira, 1985). The mass of people in the informal sector constitute a potential labour force whose presence keeps wages down within the factory gates. If existing workers demand higher wages they can always be replaced by the reserves waiting outside.

The informal sector may also keep wages down in another way, by cheapening the 'cost of labour reproduction'. The fact that the urban poor live in shanty towns may be a distinct advantage as far as employers are concerned, enabling them to pay lower wages. As Alejandro Portes and Michael Johns (1986:383) argue: "if, from the point of view of workers, unregulated housing is the way to make ends meet, from the point of view of employers, it is a means to keep wage levels at a fraction of what otherwise they would have to be." Poor housing, together with the many cheap services that are available in the poorer neighbourhoods, allows the labour force to survive and reproduce itself extremely cheaply.

But is the cost of survival cheaper in the informal economy? Victor Tokman (1978) found in the 1970s that very few products in small stores in Santiago were cheaper than in the supermarkets, and that some were distinctly dearer. The poor continued to buy from the small stores because they bought goods in small quantities, on a daily basis, and therefore store location and opening hours were critical. In addition, most small stores gave credit whereas supermarkets did not. And, while the cost of food in Bogotá's supermarkets is far higher than that charged in markets in the shanty-towns, where the poor buy most of their food, many other products that the poor consume are no cheaper locally.[3] They certainly pay more for building materials because they cannot buy in bulk. Similarly, most manufactured goods tend to cost more in small shops in the *barrios* than many modern stores. Bruno Lautier (1990:290-91) identifies an important flaw in the cheap reproduction argument when he observes that informal sector retailing is more expensive when it "concerns goods from organised industries or wholesale trade". It is only cheaper:

> when it delivers goods or services which are not offered by the formal sector; such is largely the case for housing, as well as sale of food on the streets and repair services; this role of the informal sector is not based, then, on competition with the formal sector, but rather on the capacity to move into (by producing goods of a lesser quality than those produced by the formal sector) portions of market not satisfied by the formal sector, due to lack of solvent demand.

While the modern capitalist enterprise benefits from numerous informal workers, it also faces certain disadvantages. If the labour surplus rises above the level necessary to keep down wage rates, for example, it may pose problems in terms of political or social stability. The poor may riot over social conditions, support violent political activity, or more typically, may contribute to rising crime rates. In addition, the presence of too many impoverished informal sector workers will undermine the profitability of modern companies by reducing the size of the domestic market for manufactured goods. Since the poor seek to purchase consumer durables such as

Table 4.4
Urban informal workers in labour force, 1950 and 1980

COUNTRY	1950	1980
ARGENTINA	24.3	23.0
BRAZIL	27.3	27.2
CHILE	35.1	27.1
COLOMBIA	39.0	34.4
ECUADOR	35.2	52.8
MEXICO	37.4	35.8
PERU	46.9	40.5
URUGUAY	18.6	23.1
VENEZUELA	32.1	20.8

Source: Wilkie and Perkal (1984)

radios, televisions, and bicycles, low wages will limit total demand. If every factory gains from low wages, most also lose out on limited sales.

The role of informal activity in contributing to capital accumulation is clearly not the same across different industrial sectors. While the company producing for a mass local market will suffer from the dampening effect of low wages, those producing for export or for a highly concentrated domestic market escape the negative consequences. The *maquila* on the Mexican frontier gains in every way from lower wages. The local company selling clothes to ordinary Mexicans loses out.

The informal sector: expansion or decline?

For many years the size of the informal sector was expected to decline as modernisation created jobs to replace make-do activities. In practice, the growth of the labour force and the capital-intensive form of modern industry meant that its share of the urban labour force remained disappointingly high (Table 4.4). If the informal sector declined between 1950 and 1980 in Argentina, Chile, Colombia, Mexico, Peru and Venezuela, it remained stable in Brazil, and actually increased in Ecuador and Uruguay.

If this was the situation during a period of economic expansion, what happened as a result of the recession of the 1980s?

During the 1980s modern industry and commercial activity were in severe decline. According to Tokman's (1989:37) estimate, formal sector employment increased by only 2 per cent annually between 1980 and 1985 compared to a 3.4 per cent increase in the economically active labour force. Manufacturing was particularly hard hit, with employment declining annually by 2.0 per cent. Public sector employment, where employment increased annually by 4.6 per cent, was the only 'formal' activity where jobs expanded more rapidly than the labour force. As a result of the recession, unemployment rose by 8.1 per cent per annum.

If unemployment has been rising so quickly, it suggests that the informal sector has not played the absorption role that many expected of it. Rather, as Portes (1990:32-3) argues: "The 'cushion' supposedly provided by remunerative informal activities during economic recessions turns out to be more apparent than real. ...an expanding informal sector does not counterbalance a stagnant formal sector; rather, both sectors expand and contract together."

In fact, this assessment is only partially correct. Certainly, many of the dynamic parts of the informal economy, those which offer reasonable remuneration, have declined spectacularly. But recent figures seem to support the impression one gains from the streets that the 'survival informal sector' is increasing dramatically. Tokman's (1989:37) figures clearly show that informal sector employment in nine Latin American countries increased by 6.8 per cent per annum between 1980 and 1985. Recent PREALC figures report that the contribution of the informal sector to urban employment in Latin America rose from 25.6 per cent in 1980 to 30.8 per cent in 1990, rising especially quickly in the economies most affected by recession.

Drawing on experience in Chile during the 1970s, Bruno Lautier (1990:289) shows how the informal sector expanded to sustain the poor, drawing this general conclusion:

> During periods of severe crisis, with a concurrent reduction of employment and of industrial wages, there is a growth of the informal sector, particularly among women and children. The most typical example of this situation is Chile: from 1971 to 1982, the proportion of the industrial workers in the labour force fell from 21 per cent to 11 per cent. Informal employment rose from 18 per cent (1970) to 27.2 per cent (1982): itinerant dealer-craftsmanship-services were composed of 51.8 per cent women and 22.7 per cent 12-14 year olds in 1982.

In Mexico, a similar picture is conveyed by recent anthropological work in Guadalajara and Oaxaca. In the former, Mercedes González (1990:118) claims that: "To avoid a drastic reduction in food consumption, households have sent more members to the job market; more youths, women, and children have entered the work force in order to earn the income needed for the survival of the group, the domestic unit." Helena Hirata and John Humphrey (1991:680) find similar behaviour trends among women in São Paulo, but point out that unemployed skilled men do not enter the informal sector.

Where additional workers do enter the informal sector, it is obvious that the conditions in which they work are awful. In the impoverished Mexican city of Oaxaca, for example, Henry Selby and his associates (1990:169) report that:

> informal sector activity is much reduced from 1982 levels, even though more people, especially more women, are employing themselves in these activities. There simply is not as much money around. This means that people do not have their car fixed at the local *taller*; they take their own *taco* to work with them rather than buy a *torta* at the local *lonchería*; they do not hire people to help finish off the new room in the house; and perhaps most important of all, they do not hire young people as helpers, nor care to purchase goods or services from them as they call from house to house or stand in line among the throng of shoe-shine boys in the *Zócalo*.

As a result of the recession, incomes have declined in both formal and informal activities. Between 1980 and 1991 real manufacturing wages fell by 23 per cent in both Mexico and Argentina, and average manual earnings fell by as much as 61 per cent in Lima. The value of the minimum wage fell even more dramatically; between 1980 and 1991, it had fallen by 38 per cent in Brazilian cities, 53 per cent in urban Venezuela, 57 per cent in Mexico City, and by a spectacular 83 per cent in Lima. As regards the informal sector, Ralph Hakkert and Franklin Goza (1989:74) note that "in Costa Rica, Brazil, Argentina, and Peru rapid informal sector growth during this period was associated with income declines of between 23.5 percent and 39.3 per cent." Worse still is that for many engaged in informal occupations, wages have disappeared altogether. In Mexico, "according to the National Urban Employment Survey, between 1982 and 1987 the proportion of self-employed workers and family members working without remuneration increased from 16 to 21 percent of the entire economically active population" (Cordera and González, 1990:29-30).

The situation of women

Most of the worst jobs in Latin American cities are performed by women. Certainly, most poorly paid retail jobs are done by women who dominate the stalls in the poorer markets and who also run the myriad of little shops which operate in the established shanty towns. Many hardly classify as shops in terms of their stock of merchandise, selling only ice cream, soft drinks or cigarettes. Nor is the word 'shop' really appropriate to describe what is little more than a specially adapted room in the house. The 'shop' supplements the family income while the woman performs her other domestic roles as mother and housekeeper.

Unfortunately, the recession seems to have increased women's work just at the time when incomes are falling. In Mexico, Orlandina de Oliveira and Brígida García (1990) found that the participation of women aged between twenty and forty-nine had increased from 31 percent in 1981 to 37 per cent in 1987, the height of the recession. Similarly, in the city of Querétaro, Sylvia Chant (1991:222) points out that "the growing participation of women stemmed largely from household needs to find further sources of income in the face of diminished purchasing power of existing real wages, rather than any discernible expansion in female employment opportunities." The difficulty with this argument, however, is that female participation rates were already rising before the recession. In São Paulo, for example, female participation increased more rapidly in the 1970s and in the mid-1980s, when the economy was growing, than during the deep recession of 1979-83. the rise in the proportion of women working, therefore, may be a consequence of the recession but it may also reflect a much longer-term trend.

Women are certainly less well paid then men. In Guadalajara, for example, 35.5 per cent of women earned less than one minimum salary in 1988 compared to only 16.2 per cent of men. At the other end of the earnings scale, only 4.6 per cent of women workers earned more than three minimum salaries compared to 16.1 per cent of men. Similarly, in Bogotá, whereas 53.2 per cent of women workers earned less than 35,000 pesos per month in 1989, the percentage among men was only 32.2 per cent.

Women earn less than men because they tend to do the jobs that men reject. Men are not prepared to work as domestics, an activity which employs around one-quarter of women workers in Bogotá and Lima and even more than that in La Paz. Not only are most domestic servants female, but women are excluded from the few better jobs within domestic service generally. According to Ximena Bunster and Elsa Chaney (1989:7), "men occupy the public posts in domestic service, chauffering the cars and waiting on tables, in the houses of the wealthy and in fine restaurants, while women are relegated to scrubbing pots and laundering clothes."

It is little different in commerce, the other major activity of women. Women handle the least profitable commodities and sell in the poorest markets. Nor does the situation seem much better where women have been permitted to escape their traditional roles and enter the modern manufacturing sector. Certainly, the employment conditions of women in the *maquiladoras* of Mexico in the late 1970s offered little overall improvement over their previous situation (Fernández-Kelly:1983).

Still worse, however, is the plight of women with contracts from modern enterprises to work at home. They are easily exploited by the piece-rate system and poor pay is legitimised by dominant cultural attitudes: "Practices and beliefs operating in the home and community in Latin America combine to construct gender ideologies which undervalue the work of women. Enterprises then take advantage of the cheapness of women's labour and so reinforce the ideology of undervaluation" (Lawson, 1992:17).

Child labour

If women have worse jobs than most men, the young tend to have worse jobs than most adults. Much of the scavenging, fetching and carrying in Latin American cities is done by the young. Although some casual part-time work is accepted as the norm for children in Europe and North America, child labour is much more widespread in Latin America and has become even more common as a result of the recession. In all of the region's cities there are far too many children selling chewing gum or cigarettes in the streets, far too many very young children begging, fire-eating or juggling at busy road junctions. In more affluent societies most would be at school. As Bunster and Chaney (1989:170) point out:

In an underdeveloped Third World country like Peru, urban working children contribute both to the dependent capitalist system and to the social reproduction of the labor force. They can be seen everywhere in Lima, involved in domestic and nondomestic income-generating activities. They share, in this respect, their mother's double day - a day that must be devoted to both domestic work/family maintenance and to economic activities involving petty trade and services. Many participate with their mothers fully in both.

Anybody who has visited a large Latin American city will instantly recognise that many Latin American children are forced into adult roles very early in their lives. While most middle-class children lead a comfortable existence, poorer children have to work for their living from an early age. The situation of many children is poignantly described by a young girl

THE STORY OF ANNA MARIA: A STREET SELLER IN LIMA

"I'm twelve years old and I started working in this market two years ago. My dad works as a plumber and as a bricklayer but the money he gets isn't enough to feed us all. I have six other younger brothers and sisters. My mum has to stay home with the little ones and can't go out to work. So I get up at six o'clock every morning and sell here till midday. Mum cooks some food and brings it to me so that I can eat before going to school in the afternoon.

When I started coming to this market I was very lucky because I didn't have to run after buyers - many women approached me without my having to chase them. It was my Dad who came with me for the first time and urged me to work to help feed the family. He's also the one who goes four to five times a week to the large wholesale market and buys what I'm supposed to offer at my selling place. In summer I sell vegetables or fruit, and during winter I peddle spices. In winter I have less time to study or play because when my dad brings home those assorted spices bought in bulk - cinnamon, oregano, black pepper, bay leaves, and basil - I have to sit down for hours in the evening and pack them in hundreds of little packages. Sometimes I eat my evening soup while I'm working and then go straight to bed. I'm so tired by then!

My parents pocket all the money I earn but they give me a little on Sundays so that I can go to the movies with my little brothers and sisters.

I'm worried because I don't have much time to study and I'm afraid to get stuck and fail to be promoted to sixth grade. I'm sad because things are difficult at home. Dad quarrels a lot with my Mum. How I wish the whole family to be happy without quarreling!

I like to sell because I feel I'm really working to help my parents and the little ones. Right now I'm on vacation so I've brought my little sister to be with me while I sell. I carry her on my back and she loves it!"

Source: Bunster and Chaney (1989: 174).

working on the streets of Lima.

Recently, international attention has been focused on the murder of children in Rio and other cities, and there is evidence that police, shopkeepers and other business interests are intent on removing children from the streets. According to local church and aid agencies, the plight of homeless children is now becoming a significant human rights problem.

Nevertheless, recent publicity about the problem of the 'street children' of Latin America has tended to create misleading impressions with the term used far too widely and the numbers exaggerated. UNICEF, for example, has estimated that there are 30 million street children in Latin America and 8 million in Brazil alone. The World Council of Churches has made the still more inflated claim that there are 50 million street children. Since there are roughly 150 million children under 15 in Latin America (*Economist*, 1990:27), this figure would mean that one in three children is a 'street child'. This is clearly an exaggeration and fails to distinguish between those who live on the street and those who work there. It also fails to recognise that most children are only doing odd jobs, that they may do a few hours work but also go to school.

Of course, the recession and economic crisis have led to more children working in the streets and in other forms of low-paid activity. It has also meant that in the poorer countries more have dropped out of education. In Mexico, for instance, " there have been sharp declines in high school and junior college graduation rates; in 1982-83, 42 per cent of students enrolled at these levels (persons between the ages of thirteen and nineteen) graduated; by 1985-86 that figure had been cut in half" (Cordera and González, 1991:31-2). Despite this negative trend, it is important to distinguish between different kinds of child labour. As Alec Fyfe (1989) puts it:

> Child labour is a sub-set of child work, denoting work which is exploitative of the child. Child work becomes child labour when it threatens the health and development of the children... The term 'child work' seems more appropriate when referring to the gamut of casual, small scale and part-time activities within the informal sector that provide petty-cash to an increasing number of the urban poor.

Also misleading is the assumption that child work is proof of indifference or neglect on the part of parents for this is simply not the case in most families. Indeed, Licia Valladares (1990:164) argues that child work in Rio de Janeiro is encouraged by parents as a way of protecting children from the temptations of the wider world:

> The mothers were well aware of the enticement of a life of crime. From this perspective child work acquires a new dimension. Not only does it continue to be part of an economic strategy of the household, but it also becomes a hedge against this enticement. By accustoming children to work from an early age mothers consider they are protecting them. By keeping them busy (with domestic work or casual jobs) they are keeping the child within the family and the neighbourhood circle. By encouraging them to have different work experiences they are gradually being prepared to become the expected family provider.

Even Bunster and Chaney (1989:181), whose work tends to emphasise the negative aspects of child labour, recognise that it has some positive
features: "Urban children's work is participatory in the sense that they work
for their parents, in most cases for the mother, or by themselves to
supplement the joint family income. Work itself is the training ground for
learning economic survival skills." This form of learning may appear less
desirable than a conventional education, but in a harsh economic climate it
is often the only viable course of action open to parents and children.

Notes

(1) Mohan and Hartline (1984), INEGI (1989) and OCEI (1985).

(2) 'His' is the appropriate term because very few women work as bootblacks.

(3) Bogotá's supermarkets are fascinating insofar as they appear almost to cater for
entirely different submarkets. Some, such as Olimpia, do sell more cheaply, but
others, Carulla and most notably Pulmona, sell at higher prices and rely on the
quality and packaging of their products as well as the general look of their stores to
attract higher-income customers.

Further Reading

On the culture of poverty, see Lewis (1959; 1966), on marginality, see DESAL (1969),
Germani (1973) and Perlman (1977) and on over-urbanisation, see Hoselitz (1957)
and Davis and Hertz (1954).

The United Nations Economic Commission for Latin America and the Caribbean
produces annual figures on employment and unemployment, wage levels and inflation
in Latin America. Most of the data in this chapter were drawn from this source.

On the debate about whether displaced workers remain unemployed or take up
informal sector work, see Berry (1975), Glewwe and Hall (1992), Hirata and
Humphrey (1991), Lautier (1990) and Portes (1990).

On the nature of the informal sector, see Bromley and Gerry (1979), Mazumdar (1989),
Peattie (1987), Roberts (1978) and Tokman (1989).

On the economic function of the informal sector, see Birkbeck (1979), Gilbert (1990b),
Lautier (1990), Oliveira (1985), McGee (1976) and Quijano (1974).
On household survival strategies during recession, see Chant (1991), Cordera and
González (1990), González (1990) and Selby et al. (1990).

On the role of women and children in the urban economy, see Bunster and Chaney
(1985), Chant (1991), Fernández-Kelly (1983), Hirata and Humphrey (1991) and
Valladares (1990).

5

HOUSING STRATEGIES

In 1940, most Latin American cities looked very different to the way they look today. Not only did many fewer people live in them, but they were physically much smaller. Without well-developed mass-transit systems, most people had to walk to work. Consequently, there were few suburbs and the Latin American city lacked the vast expanse of suburbia that it possesses today. Perhaps more surprising was the limited number of shanty towns - the archetypal symbol of housing in modern Latin American cities.

The city before 1950

In 1940, few families owned their homes and the vast majority were tenants. Many rented rooms in colonial-style buildings close to the city centre. A typical house was constructed on two storeys, with rooms overlooking a central patio which contained the services such as water closets and washing facilities. The precise architectural details differed between cities and between social classes, but the basic design was similar. Every income group lived in this kind of accommodation; affluent families occupied the whole house, together with their large complement of domestic servants, while poor families shared the house, each household occupying a single room.

These kinds of tenement were given local names. They were known collectively as the *vecindad* in Mexico, the *conventillo* in Bolivia, Chile, Argentina and Uruguay, the *cortijo* or *casa de comodo* in Brazil, the *callejón* in Peru, the *mesón* in El Salvador and the *inquilinato* in Colombia and Venezuela. Living conditions in the poorest tenements were often terrible; in 1919, the average Buenos Aires *inquilinato* and *conventillo* had fifteen rooms and accommodated an average of 3.3 persons per room. There were few services and repairs to the structure were infrequent. One *conventillo* in Santiago in 1941 was described as follows: "This building has 18 rooms; all flooring, stairs and roofing are in a wretched state of repair. One hundred and forty persons live in the building; fifty of them are children under fifteen years of age. Entering one dwelling place, the room seemed to be on fire, but was actually full of smoke from the cooking facilities" (Violich, 1944:70).

Few cities had large areas of self-help housing. Certain areas of huts were reported outside Santiago in the nineteenth century, and self-help areas did proliferate in Buenos Aires and Montevideo at the turn of the century, but generally self-help housing was very limited. In Rio de Janeiro, some *favelas* developed in the 1890s, but they emerged in large numbers only after 1945. In Bogotá, the residential map of 1927 shows few areas of informal housing and, in Caracas, few *barrios* had developed before 1930. In Lima, the first *barriadas* emerged in the 1920s, but there were only five in existence in 1940. Only then, did the number begin to increase exponentially: 39 by 1955, 154 in 1959, 237 in 1970, 782 in 1984.[1]

The rise of self-help housing

Today, of course, millions of people live in self-help housing and more than half of the population of many Latin American cities live in self-help neighbourhoods. Quite how much self-help housing there is depends on how this term is defined, the problem being that no-one is wholly agreed on how best to do so. Most planners, however, would probably agree that the distinctive characteristics of self-help housing is that it always begins as a rudimentary form of shelter lacking all kinds of service and is developed on land which either lacks planning permission or which has been invaded. The adjective 'self-help' stems from the fact that the occupier has built some or all of the accommodation, even if some form of professional help has almost always been involved. The typical architect is the local jobbing builder or bricklayer, and the building manual is the advice received from family and friends.

However we define 'self-help' housing, it is clear that during the post-war period a majority of poor Latin American families have been accommodated only through their own efforts. Table 5.1 illustrates for several Latin American cities how self-help shelter has become an increasingly important element in the housing solution. However dubious the data and the definitions which underpin them, the trend is clear.

The simplest explanation of the proliferation of this kind of housing is that the poor have had no alternative. With migrants pouring into the cities and with urban populations doubling every ten or fifteen years, the existing housing stock could not cope. Given generalised poverty, the highly skewed distribution of wealth, a land market that was often controlled by private monopolies and a building industry geared to formal construction methods, a 'proper' house was clearly beyond the reach of most poor families.

Rental housing in the centre of Puebla   author's photo

Wherever governments attempted to build houses for the poor they succeeded only in accommodating a minority. Given Latin American conditions, the formal building industry could keep up with the demands of the
growing middle class, but never with the needs of the majority.

But, if this argument accounts in part for the spread of self-help
housing, it is not in itself sufficient. In many other cities of the so-called
Third World, despite rapid urban growth and even lower incomes, most
poor families are tenants. Most homes in the cities of India and West Africa,
for example, are rented.[2] The expansion of self-help housing in Latin
America can only be fully explained by including three additional factors:
the development of mass transportation; the changing attitude of the state
towards informal methods of land occupation; and the growing ability of
most governments to provide services and infrastructure.

First, the expansion of self-help housing in Latin America has almost
always been associated with improvements in mass transportation. Poor
transportation meant that people were forced to live close to their work; only
when communications improved and the cost of travelling fell, did patterns
of residential location change. Buenos Aires, the pioneer of mass transportation in Latin America, was the first to experience extensive suburban
development. In 1919, the electric tram was operating over a 405-mile

Table 5.1
The growth of self-help housing in selected Latin American cities

CITY	YEAR	CITY POPULATION (000s)	POPULATION IN SQUATTER SETTLEMENTS	PERCENT
RIO DE JANEIRO	1947	2,050	400	20
	1957	2,940	650	22
	1961	3,326	900	27
	1970	4,252	1,276	30
	1991	na	na	12
MEXICO CITY	1952	2,372	330	14
	1966	3,287	1,500	46
	1970	7,314	3,438	47
	1976	11,312	5,656	50
	1990	15,783	9,470	60
LIMA	1956	1,397	112	8
	1961	1,846	347	17
	1969	3,003	805	24
	1981	4,601	1,150	25
	1991	4,805	1,778	37
BUENOS AIRES	1956	6,054	109	2
	1970	8,353	434	5
	1980	9,766	957	10
CARACAS	1961	1,330	280	21
	1964	1,590	556	35
	1971	2,200	867	39
	1985	2,742	1,673	61
RECIFE, BRAZIL	1991	na	na	42

Source: Gilbert (1990a:66), based on a variety of primary and secondary sources, supplemented by Azuela (1989:41) and Webb and Fernández (1991).

system and was carrying 3,245,000 passengers a year (Scobie, 1974). Falling fares allowed workers to join the middle class in the move to the suburbs, and self-help housing became common. Elsewhere, however, there were few effective public transport systems before 1940. Horse-drawn trams were still operating in Rio de Janeiro in 1926, and there were still only 550 electric trams operating in São Paulo as late as 1934. The growth of suburbia awaited the coming of the bus. In São Paulo, "the bus lines made it possible to link up even the most distant residential areas with the workplace. This in turn led to intense property speculation, as unoccupied land was transformed into plots to be sold off to the droves of workers coming in the wake of industrial expansion" (Kowarick and Ant, 1988:10). Mexico City, which had only 1,600 buses in 1935, experienced something similar; as the numbers of buses increased, so did the size of the city. Mexico City virtually doubled its area between 1940 and 1950, that of Guadalajara increased seven fold between 1920 and 1960, and Bogotá's grew more than three fold in the 1940s and 1950s.

Second, the spread of self-help housing was only permitted by the benign attitude of the state. In the past, planning ordinances had been approved which banned the development of such forms of shelter. While planners continued to declare the development of unserviced land illegal, in practice the authorities increasingly turned a blind eye. In some cities governments even allowed poor families to invade state land. In Lima, Rio de Janeiro, Salvador, Caracas, Guayaquil and Barranquilla vast swathes of public land were occupied 'illegally' with the tacit approval of the authorities. Elsewhere, landowners were not punished for subdividing their land, despite the lack of services and planning permission. Of course, there were moments when governments attempted to stem the tide of self-help suburbia, but these were not common. The simple fact was that self-help housing represented a means by which the poor could be accommodated at little cost to the state. It was politically expedient to ignore the government's own planning regulations. The state not only tolerated self-help housing but encouraged its development through the gradual introduction of services and infrastructure. Water taps, electricity lines, schools and clinics slowly trickled into the self-help suburbs.

Third, the servicing of low-income settlements was made possible by improved technology and increasing government budgets. Modern engineering provided the means to generate and distribute electricity and water. Industrial and commercial development provided governments with funds to expand their education and health systems. However deficient the servicing of the low-income areas, something was done to placate their inhabitants and to prevent the spread of epidemics.

Figure 5.1
Social segregation in Bogotá: the incidence of poverty in 1985

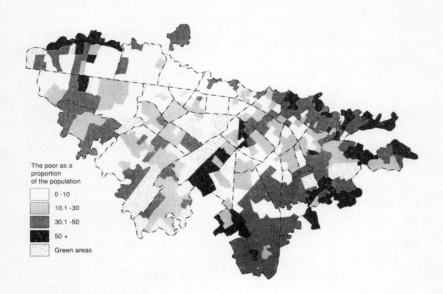

The poor as a
proportion
of the population

	0 -10
	10.1 -30
	30.1 -50
	50 +
	Green areas

Acquiring land

As a general rule, rich and poor live in different areas of the Latin American
city (Figure 5.1). The rich choose their preferred locales and the poor
occupy the land that is left over, usually in the least attractive parts of the
city. The poor of La Paz occupy the cold inhospitable land of El Alto, 1,200
feet above the city centre and over 2,000 feet above the select neighbourhoods of the elite. The poor of Guayaquil occupy homes built on stilts above
the tidal swamps to the south and the west of the city. The poor of Lima build
their homes on desert land that is too distant or too desolate to be of any
commercial interest.

   If the general pattern is similar between cities, there has been a great
deal of variation. In one city, the poor would be allowed to invade land, in
another, invasions would be vigorously opposed. In one city, land could be
obtained without cost, elsewhere it would be sold by private developers at
a price equivalent to unserviced land in the more prosperous parts of the city.
The particular form of land occupation that has developed depends upon the

local pattern of land ownership, the price of peripheral land, the attitude of the political authorities, the political organisation of the poor, the physical nature of the terrain, and the pace of urban growth.

Perhaps the most critical element has been the reaction of the state. In places, the authorities were fully prepared to tolerate invasions or illegal forms of settlement. In São Paulo, "Governor Ademar de Barros made no bones about it when in 1946 he told the poor: 'Go ahead and build your homes without a permit. City Hall will turn a blind eye'" (Kowarick and Bonduki, 1988:6). Elsewhere the authorities did not share this attitude. Sometimes, when the government changed in a city, so did the form of land allocation. In Caracas, whereas a civilian government allowed self-help settlements to occupy state land between 1945 and 1948, the military regime of Marcos Pérez Jiménez (1948-57) strongly opposed the growth of shanty towns and launched a war on the *ranchos*. With the return of democratic rule in 1958, the policy towards self-help housing changed again. Similarly, in Rio de Janeiro, the military regime which took power in 1964 launched a programme of *favela* removal which contrasted strongly with earlier, more tolerant, attitudes. By 1983, however, a populist governor in search of votes was again initiating a programme promising "a plot for every family".

Poor families have hardly been passive bystanders in this political game. By pressurising the authorities they have been able to improve their chances of obtaining land. Of course, their leaders had to be well-organised and had to understand the local political situation. In Ciudad Guayana in the 1960s, for example, potential squatters had to be very diligent in their research; land belonging to the National Housing Bank was fair game for invasion but not that belonging to the Development Corporation (Daykin, 1978:348-9). The invasion of peripheral land might well be permitted in general, but not the occupation of land reserved for some special project favoured by the mayor or state governor. Sometimes even private land could be occupied, especially that belonging to foreigners or members of the political opposition. Much clearly depended on the relations between the leader and the authorities. Since the authorities would often be divided in their reaction to an invasion, success might well depend on the leader's contacts. If these had influence with the police, repression might be avoided; if not, reprisals could be swift.

Building a home

Most pictures of self-help housing which appear in the media show a primitive shelter built out of cardboard, corrugated iron or bamboo. Some academic accounts have also sometimes assumed that low-income settlements contain nothing but shacks. Frank Bonilla (1970), for example, stated that three million of Rio de Janeiro's inhabitants in 1960 "lived within these

A LAND INVASION IN LIMA

The following description comes from Mangin (1970a: 50-52). It describes the invasion of land in Lima during the 1950s in which a waiter, called Blas, and his wife, Carmen, were principal actors. An example from Lima is appropriate because land invasions have been common in that city for many years and much of the early enthusiasm for self-help housing was based on work conducted in Peru. The choice of an example from the 1950s is influenced by the fact that, from 1950 until 1956, the military dictator who ruled Peru had been surreptitiously encouraging land invasions. He had done this in order to undermine the support of the poor from his principal political opponents, the APRA party. In any case, the process of invasion as described here differs little from those described for later periods of Lima's history or indeed from those that occur in other Latin American cities.

The example illustrates clearly how organised invasion groups were in mounting the occupation of the land, how careful they were in selecting the participants, and how they sought to win support from powerful political figures and public sympathy for their cause.

"A colleague of Blas's in the restaurant had spoken to him about a group to which he belonged. The members were organising an invasion of state land to build houses and they wanted fifty families. The group had been meeting irregularly for about a year and when Blas was invited they had forty of the fifty that they sought.

The waiter's group came mainly from the same central highland region and their spokesman and leader was a bank employee who was also a functionary of the bank employees' union. The other major faction was a group of career army enlisted men, including several members of a band that plays at state functions, who were stationed near the proposed invasion site.

They met a few times with never more than fifteen men present. They were encouraged by the fact that the government seemed to be tolerating squatter invasions. Several earlier invasion attempts had been blocked by the police and in many barriadas people had been beaten, some shot, and a few killed. The recent attitude, in 1954, seemed tolerant, but their invasion was illegal.

Many barriada invasions had been arranged for the eve of a religious or national holiday. The next holiday was the Independence Day vacation, July 28th, 29th, 30th; so they picked the night of the 27th. It would give them a holiday to provide a patriotic aura as well as three days off from work to consolidate their position. They thought of naming their settlement after the dictator's popular wife, but, after taking into account the vicissitudes of current politics, they decided to write to her about their pitiful plight, but to name the place after a former general-dictator, long dead, who freed the slaves.

A letter was drawn up for mailing to the dictator's wife and for presentation to the press. The letter stressed equally their respect for the government and their abandonment by the government.

During the last month word was passed from the active meeting-goers, still never more than 20 or 25, to the others and preparations were made. Each family bought its own straw mats and poles for the house, and small groups made arrangements for trucks and taxis. Each household was asked to get a Peruvian flag or make one out of paper. No two remember the details of the invasion the same way, but about thirty of the expected forty-five families did invade during the night. A newspaper photographer was notified by the invaders and he arrived about the time the houses were being finished. The members had discussed previously what lots they would take, and how the streets were to be laid out and there was very little squabbling during the first day. By early morning when the police arrived there were at least thirty one-room straw houses flying Peruvian flags and the principal streets were outlined with stones.

The police told them they would have to leave. A picture and story appeared in two papers and by the 30th of July about twenty or thirty more families had come, including some of the old members. A few men, with the help of friends and relatives and, in at least one case, paid workers, had built brick walls around their lots. They were told to leave several times but no one forced them. A resident, not one of the original invaders, was killed by the police in 1960 during an attempt to build a school on government land. The unfavourable publicity caused the government to desist and the residents cut a lot out of the hillside and built a school.

Blas and Carmen picked a lot about fifteen by thirty metres on the gradual slope of the hill on the principal street. The lot was somewhat larger than most subsequent lots, an advantage of being an original invader.

Blas and some friends quickly expanded the simple invasion one-room house to a three-room straw mat house, and they outlined the lot with stones. He worked hard on Sundays and some nights, sometimes alone, sometimes with friends from the *barriada* or outside. He soon managed to get a brick wall six-and-a-half feet high round his property."

jerry-built, vertical islands of squalor".

Although basic shelters clearly exist in large numbers, they are hardly representative of the bulk of Latin America's self-help housing. The shack is the first attempt of a family to house itself and is normally put up during the first days of a land invasion when the settlers are more anxious to demonstrate their presence to the authorities than to keep out the wind and rain. Admittedly, some shelters do not look much better a few years later although these are usually located either in hot areas or in settlements which are being harassed by the authorities. Where the climate is hot, homes tend to be much flimsier because brick or cement walls are not needed to keep out the cold. The main requirement is that the roof does not leak when it rains. Rudimentary shelter is also found in settlements whose tenure is insecure. If the authorities continue to threaten a community then the residents will not attempt to improve their dwellings, since there is little point if the police will destroy the improvements. A few settlements are always under threat somewhere in Latin America.

Such cases apart, however, the majority of Latin American self-help homes improve through time. Once the settlers know that they will be left alone, they begin to consolidate. They do not need title deeds to the land, as some international agencies tend to argue, but simply want signs of good intent from the authorities. The offer of electricity or water, the removal of a police barrier from the main road into the settlement, even a friendly visit from the mayor or a councillor will suffice. With such a vote of confidence behind them, work gets underway. Wooden or corrugated iron shacks may front some plots but a concrete and brick room will usually be under construction behind. The owners, especially if someone in the family is involved in the building industry, will spend their spare time constructing the permanent home. If they do not have the required expertise, then they will obtain advice and assistance from neighbours and kin. There is a huge pool of self-help 'know-how' in Latin American shanty towns and a large number of jobbing builders to give advice. When the owners do not know how to undertake some special task, they always have the option of employing an expert to do it for them. The plumbing and electrics will often be installed in this way. Some tasks require a lot of hands, and here the neighbours will usually help. Installing a concrete roof over the weekend is a regular, cooperative activity. An atmosphere of gaiety, often assisted by a crate of beer, will accompany the collective effort.

The result of the settlers' hard work is that whole settlements are gradually transformed from ramshackle structures into consolidated neighbourhoods. Of course, some families proceed much faster than others. The critical ingredient for improving a house is money, both to buy the materials and to hire labour.[3] Families with savings can consolidate their homes surprisingly quickly. Those who lack funds remain in a basic hut or fail to

A real shanty: shack in
Buenos Aires, Guadalajara
(above) Decorated two-
storey house in Agustín
Yañez, Guadalajara (left)
author's photos

move into the settlement at all, continuing to share or rent accommodation somewhere else. But, where the process of consolidation is working well, amazingly speedy transformations take place. The photographs on page 89 show houses at different stages of consolidation in one settlement in Guadalajara. The hut belongs to new arrivals. Along the route to improvement it may be followed by a concrete house; complete with reinforcing bars it will withstand the most severe earthquake. Eventually, a second storey may be built on, a balcony constructed and decorative tiling attached .

Gradually, what began as a sea of shanties becomes a consolidated settlement. Electricity and water are installed, the roads are paved, bus services begin operating and schools are built. The visual signs of progress are often dramatic. The photographs opposite show the same street in Atenas (Bogotá) in 1979 and 1992. In 1979, although street lighting had recently been installed and water had been available for some time the settlement still looked like a shanty town. By 1992, however, the streets had been paved, the houses had become much more consolidated, and the earlier temporary street lights had been replaced by lamps on concrete posts. Atenas had been transformed and was no longer a shanty town.

The struggle for services

Adequate shelter requires more than just a roof and walls, it also requires services. Initially, a community may steal what it needs. Tapping into the water lines is a regular practice and linking a transformer to the electricity mains is an easy task for a local electrician. Once the main supply has been obtained, a provisional water or electricity network can be established. A tangle of wires hanging like spaghetti from electricity poles is a common sight in most Latin American cities.

Such a solution is hardly satisfactory. Provisional electricity networks are easily overloaded, provide too low a voltage and are also likely to be damaged during storms. Informal water networks operate at low pressure and are therefore likely to leak and allow impurities into the system. Such solutions are also unpopular with the utility companies who lose revenue and often have to clear up the damage caused by the improvised connections. Sometimes the companies demolish illegal connections; at best they come to an agreement with the settlement to provide an official service.

Unfortunately, it is often difficult to convince the authorities to provide services. Few urban governments in Latin America have adequate resources, many are less than well organised and all are struggling against the rapid expansion of new residential areas. When we recall that, during the 1970s, Mexico City and São Paulo each had some 300,000 people added to their populations every year, we have to have some sympathy with the

Unconsolidated street in Atenas, Bogotá in 1979 (above) The same street 13 years later (below)
author's photos

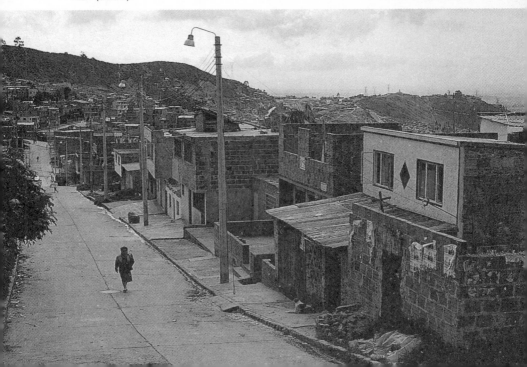

authorities.

As a result, obtaining services is a real struggle. In many cities, it requires insistent petitioning by settlement leaders. They must constantly visit the offices of public officials, councillors and political allies to remind them of the settlement's continued existence and the seriousness of its needs. Since servicing is part of the day-to-day process of partisan politicking, settlements which support the party in power tend to be more successful. The timing of petitioning can be critical, for while many services are handed out before elections, few are delivered between campaigns. Many self-help settlers complain that politicians always appear a few days before the ballot, only to disappear when they have been elected.

Even when politicians come to the settlements it may make little difference. Two councillors in Bogotá used to visit low-income settlements lacking water. "Vote for us and we will get you water", was the implicit promise. The truth was somewhat different. They had seen the plans of the water company, knew where it was going to lay the pipes and were merely promising water to settlements which were going to get serviced anyway.[4]

Sometimes, however, petitioning does not work and the authorities ignore a community. In other cases the settlement leaders are instructed to keep their constituents quiet and are rewarded with jobs or political advancement. Sometimes, the settlement is known to have supported the wrong political party and is punished with neglect. Occasionally, the settlement has occupied land that the authorities want for some other purpose; the settlement is not serviced in an attempt to discourage consoli-

Table 5.2
The development of owner occupation in selected cities since 1950
(Percent of households owning their home)

CITY	1950/2	1960/1	1970/1	1980/2
MEXICO CITY	27	23	43	64
GUADALAJARA	29	28	43	52
PUEBLA	36	16	39	48
CARACAS	47	45	52	64
LIMA	na	17	42	48
SANTIAGO, CHILE	26	37	57	64

Source: Gilbert (1993); Riofrío (1978: 58); INE (1986)

Rental housing in a consolidated self-help area in Guadalajara   author's photo

dation and to keep down the cost of any subsequent compensation. Under such circumstances, the settlers have to resort to more disruptive methods.

The most common reaction to neglect is simply to organise a mass visit to the government's offices. Few officials welcome the arrival of several hundred people, especially when the community is accompanied by a couple of opportunistic politicians. If mass petitioning does not work, and the situation becomes desperate, then it is not unknown for people to return to throw stones at the office windows. But, on the whole, violence is risky, is no guarantee of success and can be dangerous for the participants. Even when wives and children accompany the protesters, the police may retaliate.

Owners, tenants and sharers

A much higher proportion of families own their own house today than was the case twenty or thirty years ago. They may not have full legal title to the land but everyone respects their *de facto* tenure rights. Figures from a variety of cities show how quickly owner-occupation has expanded in Latin America during the post-war period (Table 5.2).

If tenants have declined as a percentage of urban inhabitants, their numbers have not and, in some cities, they have increased substantially. Despite the growth of owner-occupation, the number of non-owner families

---

PORTRAIT OF A LANDLORD

Pablo Núñez and his wife Amelia own one property in Puebla (Mexico), where they live with two tenant households and two of their married children. They are an elderly couple with six other grown-up children. Pablo is a retired textile worker, receiving a pension worth about half of the minimum salary. Both he and his wife still work as traders, selling a variety of goods. They have not been doing very well recently, as Amelia quickly gets tired. As a result, they depend fairly heavily on the rents from the two rented flats., which total about three-quarters of the minimum salary. Occasionally, they have been unable to buy food because their tenants have not paid the rent.

Before moving here, the couple had always lived in *vecindades*, which they hated. They jumped at the chance to buy this plot, 35 years ago. They built one room plus a kitchen and came to live in Veinte de Noviembre straight away. Over the years, they gradually added the rest of the building, including the two flats now occupied by the tenants. The second rented flat had taken five or six years to build, because they were short of money. Eventually, under pressure from people wanting to rent the unfinished rooms, they had taken out a loan to complete the work.

Renting is not a good business. Pablo wanted to sell up but Amelia would not let him: the rent would eke out their income and the property was something to leave to the family. The two children who are living on the plot pay no rent. One is unemployed and the other recently got married and is saving up to buy furniture for his own house; neither can spare anything at the moment.

Source: Gilbert and Varley (1991: 156-7).

---

in Mexico City increased from 484,000 in 1950 to 1.2 million in 1980.

Where are these tenants living? The answer, in part, is where they have always done: in the central city. This remains the typical tenant location, and a higher proportion of households in the central city are tenants than anywhere else. But over time, urban renewal has seen the demolition of many central tenements and new rental accommodation has been required. This has been provided by what at first sight may appear to be an odd source. The new accommodation has been created in older self-help housing areas by owners who originally built their own dwellings. On the whole, the new rental property is not in the newest and most peripheral self-help areas. It tends to appear in settlements which have well-developed services and infrastructure and, especially, in those which are located conveniently close to areas of work or which at least have good transport links.

The new landlords do not fit the archetypal image of rich slumlords with large numbers of properties. On the whole, recent research shows that the landlords own little in the way of property and that they seldom have more than ten or so tenants. It also shows that few landlords have a good business sense and that most would probably have made much more money had they invested in stocks and shares, indulged in dollar speculation or simply put their money in the bank. They have often become landlords because they believe in the stability of bricks and mortar. They do not trust modern financial systems and they want something to leave to their children.

It would be wrong to suggest that such people always make generous and caring landlords. But when tenants are asked about their relations with the landlord, few have many complaints. Indeed, the overwhelming impression gained from interviews in the consolidated self-help settlements is that the relationship between landlords and tenants is relatively benign. Landlords do evict tenants, especially when the latter do not pay the rent or when the landlord needs the property, but evictions are not all that common. In many cities, tenants live a long time in the same property; in Santiago the average is six years, in Guadalajara eight years and in Puebla nine. In some cities, too, rents are often remarkably low, since many landlords seem reluctant to put up the rents of sitting tenants.

Long tenures are most common in the central areas where many tenants have lived for twenty or thirty years in the same home. Here, however, landlord-tenant relations are less amicable. Tenant organisations are often active and landlords are sometimes anxious to sell their property. No doubt part of the reason why relations are less friendly is that rent controls have kept rents very low and landlords are reluctant to maintain property for which they are receiving little in rent.

Since most tenants reply that they would one day like to be owners, why do they not move into the consolidating self-help areas? The answer in some places is that they cannot afford to do so, particularly in those cities where even unserviced plots of land have to be purchased. Saving the money to buy a plot takes time and aspiring home-owners often remain as tenants while they are accumulating the deposit. Even when they have bought the plot, they may have too little money to build the house.

But not all tenants are too poor to become owners. Some do have enough money to buy land and building materials and even to hire paid labour to help in the task of construction. Such tenants have often decided that they do not want to live in an unserviced settlement. If this is the only kind of ownership they can afford, they prefer to remain as tenants. Faced by the choice of building their own house in a distant, poorly serviced settlement or remaining as a tenant in a properly serviced neighbourhood, close to work and to the homes of friends and family, the decision comes easily.

Of course, some poor families simply have no choice. Where incomes are low and rents are rising, non-payment of the rent may lead to eviction. Here the family may well take the opportunity to move into an invasion settlement or to buy a cheap plot however distant the neighbourhood.

But what happens in cities where rents are high and plots are expensive? One answer is that some families are able neither to own nor to rent. Their only 'choice' is to share a home with relatives or friends. Under the Pinochet regime, this became a very common response in Santiago, a city where neither land invasions nor illegal subdivisions were permitted. And although the Chilean government offered generous housing subsidies to poor families, many households were simply too poor to qualify for inclusion in the scheme. Since rental housing has been in decline in Santiago for many years, and rent controls were dismantled during the 1980s, rents are high relative to incomes. As a result, the number of sharers, known locally as *allegados* has risen hugely. As many as one family in five may have been living in shared accommodation in Santiago in 1983.

Not every family that shares accommodation, however, is an economic refugee. Indeed, some families deliberately choose to share, at least on a temporary basis. The big advantage of sharing is that no rent has to be paid. Another advantage is that there is sometimes more space available in the parental home than in a rented room. There can also be social advantages, particularly for single-parent families. Living with parents offers a built-in baby-sitting service for the grandchildren; it also offers families a way of pooling their incomes. It can also provide a necessary refuge for women in a male-dominated world, in which the traditions of *machismo* do not always produce sober, pacific and caring husbands. Whether they choose this option or whether they are forced into it, Sylvia Chant (1991:223) is probably right when she argues that some women are much better off living without a man.

Self-help housing: solution or exploitation?

There has long been a debate between academics, planners and politicians about the merits of self-help as a housing 'solution'. For years, of course, the official attitude towards so-called 'squatter' housing was highly negative. Politicians did not like to see their cities developing what they considered to be a form of social cancer. Self-help settlements were clearly slums, inhabited by ignorant peasants, newly arrived, in excessive numbers, direct from the countryside. Planners and architects were appalled by the lack of services and infrastructure, and by the primitive construction methods employed by the informal builders. Academics were also critical, viewing such settlements as a sign that people were moving to the city before there was sufficient work to provide them with satisfactory incomes. Such migrants were being attracted by the 'bright lights' of the city, they were failing to make an informed decision about the advisability of leaving their rural home. Both academics and planners argued that such settlements were full of people 'marginal' to the real urban economy. As Barbara Ward (1964) put the case:

> The unskilled poor are streaming away from subsistence agriculture, to exchange the squalor of rural poverty for the even deeper miseries of the shanty towns. They are the core of local despair and disaffection undermining the all too fragile structure of public order and thus retarding the economic development that alone can help their plight.

Janice Perlman (1976) shows how such ideas were frequently cited by the more affluent and powerful as reasons why cityward migration should be discouraged and why self-help settlements should be destroyed.

'Enlightened' planners sought to remedy the evils of slum housing by recommending its replacement with proper houses. Thousands of homes were built by governments throughout the region in a vain effort to accommodate the poor. In practice, the majority of such homes were too expensive and most were claimed by government workers, trade unionists and supporters of the party or group in power. In any case, there were simply too many poor families to be accommodated in this way. Governments built too expensively to house the poor and, if they introduced subsidies, they simply ran out of funds. Many ended up building too few homes at standards which were beyond the resources of the poor. Others constructed what most people considered to be official slums - tiny concrete cells built on small plots, miles from the centre of town.

Such negative attitudes to self-help housing have never disappeared, and antipathy towards it continues to be expressed in every Latin American city today. But, gradually, the criticism became less trenchant. Politicians began to realise that the urban poor did vote and that there was a large potential electorate in the squatter settlements waiting to be wooed. In any case, both planners and politicians were increasingly aware that there was no real alternative. Migrants were not going to stay in the countryside, so something had to be done to accommodate them. Since governments could not build enough houses, and there was not enough rental accommodation, the only feasible option was to allow the poor to house themselves.

At the same time, there was increasing evidence during the 1960s that the poor did not too bad a job. Research showed that many in the squatter settlements had regular jobs. Most of the inhabitants had been living in the city for some time and were well adjusted to urban life. These people were not suffering from social anomie: they led regular family lives, they knew something about the political situation, and, when permitted, they actually cast votes. The so-called 'culture of poverty' was either a figment of Oscar Lewis's imagination or a result of his peculiar research method.

Particularly impressive were the results of the poor's efforts at architecture. Their housing stood up during earthquakes when many a government building fell down. Their housing design might be rudimentary in terms of the latest architectural theories, but it worked nevertheless. Most important was that the design of their housing matched their needs. Rather than the poor building slums, they built houses that were often better adjusted to their family requirements than the homes designed by professionals. They extended their homes when they needed more space, they built accommodation which could help supplement their incomes - a shop at the front or a workshop at the side. At the very least, unlike many government homes, the housing they built was affordable. As a result of studying these efforts, a group of architects and planners, including Charles Abrams, William Mangin and John Turner, began to argue that self-help housing was an architecture that worked. Rather than constituting slums, shanty towns represented a potential solution to the housing problem.

According to this theory, governments should let the poor build their own homes and assist them by performing the jobs that can only be done adequately on a large scale. Thus instead of building houses, governments should build the roads, provide the water and electricity, and supply school teachers and health workers. Such an approach would avoid debacles such as that wrought by the Venezuelan dictator, Marcos Pérez Jiménez, when he waged his war on the *ranchos* in Caracas. Not only did the former inhabitants of the self-help settlements resent being forced into government-built apartment blocks, which they were ill-disposed to look after and which quickly deteriorated, but they also became politically active and helped to depose him.

As a result of this new kind of thinking, more and more governments began to upgrade rather than destroy self-help settlements. Some even began to develop sites-and-service projects to accommodate the huge number of newly established families. While upgrading tended to work rather well, sites-and-services schemes were less successful. Governments were not very effective in providing cheap sites for the projects and the total cost of a plot and its core house was too often beyond the budget of a poor family. In addition, few sites-and-services schemes were developed in the larger Latin American cities. Nevertheless, by the 1970s, the new conventional wisdom was well established and was being supported extensively by funds from the international development and aid agencies.

It was around this time that the political Left launched a major offensive against self-help housing. State support for self-help housing, it was argued, was totally misguided because it rested on a misunderstanding of the nature of the housing problem. Homelessness could not be resolved except through a radical restructuring of society. Burgess (1982) is a strong advocate of this argument and favourably cites Engels (1872:74) in support of his case:

> As long as the capitalist mode of production continues to exist it is folly to hope for an isolated settlement of the housing question affecting the lot of the workers. The solution lies in the capitalist mode of production and the appropriation of all the means of subsistence and the instruments of labour by the working class itself.

The essential thesis of writers such as Burgess and Pradilla (1978) was that encouraging the poor to build their own homes was an attack on their living standards. In a decent society, employers would pay wages that covered the costs of a proper shelter for their workers. To encourage self-help was a means of reducing the cost of the 'reproduction of labour' and a way of undermining the need to pay a proper wage. The new thinking, it was claimed, also freed governments from their obligation to house their citizens adequately. Workers should have the right to proper housing without having to build them in their free time. By encouraging self-help construction, governments would withdraw from what was their moral duty to society.

These critics also attacked the effectiveness of a self-help shelter strategy in providing a housing solution. The essential problem lay in the nature of the state. Why should undemocratic governments, which supported policies which did nothing to redress the unfairness inherent in most Latin American societies, introduce policies which would help the poor? In order to introduce sites-and-services schemes on a large scale, something had to be done about the price of urban land. Would governments begin to control land speculation and thereby help the poor buy a plot of land? Would governments increase taxes so as to help subsidise services and create the services and infrastructure required to allow self-help housing to flourish? The answer was clearly no.

Even the doyen of self-help advocates, John Turner, who came under strong attack from such critics, had severe doubts about the efficacy of what was happening on the ground. In 1976 and 1982 he argued that he had been misunderstood and that he supported collective efforts at self-help rather than the individual efforts of millions of poor families. If communities hired professional help and bought materials in bulk, they would produce better housing more cheaply than through their individual efforts. Efforts should be made to encourage a cooperative spirit among the poor.

Clearly, self-help housing will remain the norm for the bulk of poor families in Latin America. For those living in cities where the economy manages to grow, self-help will continue to be a difficult, but feasible, route to housing improvement. No-one would claim that families who work long hours for low wages should have to build their own homes in their limited spare time. But, in a sometimes harsh reality, it is a better answer than most of the alternatives. Today, there is general acceptance among most governments and lending agencies that self-help settlements should generally be left in place. A great deal of money is being spent on providing these settlements with services and infrastructure. Governments are now mostly willing to provide legal title to the land, sometimes even when it has been invaded. In Chile, Mexico and Venezuela, major legalisation campaigns have been introduced during the last few years.

Nevertheless, serious doubts surround the current conventional wisdom on housing which relies so heavily on market forces. The latest World Bank (1993) policy document on housing, for example, is subtitled 'enabling markets to work'. The first principle guiding the Bank's future assistance in the housing sector is to "encourage government to play an enabling role: to move away from producing, financing, and maintaining housing, and toward improving housing market efficiency and the housing conditions of the poor" (World Bank, 1992a:7). It is argued that the private sector, whether in the formal or the informal sector, can improve housing better than the state. Not only does this mean that government should generally leave construction to the private sector, but also that the state should intervene less through the imposition of planning regulations and controls. According to the Bank, in most countries of Latin America, the "priorities are fiscal and financial policy reform, particularly improving housing finance institutions and reducing budgetary transfers to the housing sector, and expanding infrastructure investment." While no-one who has studied state intervention in the housing market in Latin America will regret a certain rolling back of its role, the current statements from Washington sound all too much like 'trickle-down' economics. Will the benefits really reach the majority of the poor?

It is possible that this approach will be effective in the expanding economies of the region. If poor people find work and their incomes start to rise, then they will be able to improve the quality of their homes. If more and cheaper credit is made available, the operation of land and housing markets may well improve to everyone's benefit. If government, or increasingly private enterprise, invests in sensible projects, the quality and availability of infrastructure and services may improve for increasing numbers of low-income settlers. But so much depends on continued economic growth and on its more equitable distribution. In the region's declining economies, or those where the distribution of income continues to deteriorate, market forces will not help poor families to improve their shelter. Not only does economic decline cut family budgets, but it also undermines the ability of governments to supply services. Self-help settlement with water, electricity and sewerage is one thing; its development without such basic amenities is hardly to be commended. It is an unfortunate fact that during the economic recession of the 1980s many governments cut back investment in just this area of activity. It remains to be seen whether the experience of the 1990s will be significantly better.

Notes

(1) The data relating to Santiago come from de Ramón (1985); for Buenos Aires from Scobie (1974); for Rio de Janeiro from Morse (1965); for Caracas from Morris (1978); for Lima from Matos Mar (1968), Lloyd (1981), Riofrío (1978) and Dietz (1987).

(2) Peil and Sada (1984); Tipple and Willis (1991); India, NIUA (1989).

(3) See Ward (1976) for a detailed account of the relationship between savings and housing improvement in Mexico City.

(4) For a detailed account of this process, see Gilbert and Ward (1985).

Further reading

Good accounts of urban housing in the nineteenth and early twentieth centuries are provided in Hahner (1986), Kowarick and Ant (1988), Morse (1958), Scobie (1974), de Ramón (1985) and Violich (1944).

The process of land acquisition in different Latin American cities is well explained by the following: Avello *et al.* (1989), Collier (1976), Carroll (1980), Carroll (1980), Cleaves (1974), Daykin (1978), Eckstein (1990), Gilbert and Ward (1985), Kusnetzoff (1975), Mangin (1970a), Ray (1969) and Sachs (1990).

For accounts of recent research on rental housing in Latin American cities, see Camacho and Terán (1991), Coulomb and Sánchez (1991), Gilbert and Varley (1991), Gilbert (1993) and Van Lindert (1991).

On shared housing, see Chant (1985), Gilbert (1993) and Ogrodnik (1983).

For accounts of how competently migrants adapted to the city, see Butterworth (1962), Cornelius (1975), Mangin (1967 and 1970b), Perlman (1976) and Portes (1972).

The argument that self-help housing was a viable housing 'solution' is described in Abrams (1964), Mangin (1967, 1970b) and Turner (1967 and 1968). A radical critique is offered by Pradilla (1976) and Burgess (1978). Much of this critique was directed at John Turner who replied in Turner (1976 and 1982). Further discussion of self-help housing are included in Ward (ed.) (1982) and Mathey (1992).

6

URBAN MANAGEMENT

To most people the phrase 'urban management in Latin America' sounds like a contradiction in terms. Everyone knows that Latin America's cities are badly run. Don't Latin American cities suffer from a gamut of urban horrors, from slums and shanty towns through to air pollution and inadequate sewerage systems? Are the authorities not corrupt? Most Latin Americans would agree that their cities are anything but well run. Even public officials bemoan the ills of their administration and only new incumbents speak optimistically about the prospects for reform. Better urban management, by their administration, will sweep the stables clean. Unfortunately, such reforming zeal seldom lasts for long and they end up condemning the unbeatable, unreformable and unjustifiable systems like everyone else.

In this universal accord about the weaknesses of urban management in Latin America one important point is in danger of being forgotten. If urban administration is as bad as has been described, how have so many Latin American cities managed to absorb such large numbers of people without having suffered either a major disaster or a social revolution? If the administration in Mexico City has been as bad as it is painted, how did it manage to accommodate five million additional people during the 1970s? How would the authorities in London, Paris or New York have managed if five million more people had been added to their cities' populations within a decade? Despite the often justified horror stories, urban government in Latin America has generally coped. Services and infrastructure have been extended and have generally kept up with the booming populations. Of course, there has been waste, corruption and incompetence, but a great deal has been achieved nonetheless. Without some degree of competence, the lid would have blown off the urban pot long ago.

The argument of this chapter is that urban management in much of Latin America is bad but could be much worse. The lesson, I believe, is not that Latin Americans are incompetent managers but that the social, economic and political context in which they are expected to do their jobs makes any accomplishment extremely difficult. Many of the problems are caused by a lack of resources. When money is scarce, governments do not pay their bills; when it is very scarce, they do not even pay their employees. As a result, neither contractors nor employees work very hard. When wages are too low, employees moonlight, supplementing their incomes with outside work. However competent an incoming mayor or governor, there is little that can be done if insufficient resources are available. It is difficult, for example, to run an urban government without adequate funding and that was precisely the problem during the recession-racked 1980s. Many of the improvements that had been made in Latin American urban administration during the 1970s have been undone by the stringencies of coping with the debt crisis.

Services and infrastructure

Before 1940, few Latin American cities were very large or contained much in the way of industry. As a result, they could survive with fairly rudimentary infrastructure systems. Public transport facilities were poor, electricity and water services were limited, and there were no sewerage systems in most areas of the city. After 1940, the rapid growth of Latin America's cities placed vast new demands on their governments. As their populations grew, they required, and sometimes demanded, major improvements in the availability and quality of services. Both rich and poor expected better roads, a more reliable electricity system, potable water and decent health services. Better infrastructure was also essential if industrial and commercial development was to be sustained.

In response to this need, impressive improvements were made to key services in many cities. The annual consumption of electricity in Mexico City increased from 682 megawatts in 1930 to 20,267 megawatts in 1984. In Caracas, the number of telephone subscribers increased from 12,000 in 1931 to 205,000 in 1966. In Bogotá, electricity generation increased from 53,000 Kw/hours in 1936 to 700,000 in 1960.

Such rapid rates of expansion led to an overall improvement in service provision. Indeed, as William Dixon (1987) shows, the provision of infrastructure and services in 1980 had never been better. While the situation varied greatly from service to service, there is no doubt that water, sewerage and electricity delivery had generally improved. Table 6.1 compares the proportions of the urban population receiving water, sewerage and electricity in a number of Latin American countries in 1960 and 1980. Although the situation in 1960 was rather poor, and the improvement in sewerage services in Argentina, Costa Rica and Guatemala still left the majority without sanitation, the overall trend is very clear.

Table 6.1
Urban service delivery in selected Latin American countries
(per cent with service)

COUNTRY	SEWERAGE		WATER		ELECTRICITY	
	1960	1980	1960	1980	1960	1980
ARGENTINA	65	68	42	40	85	95
BRAZIL	55	80	55d	32	73	88
CHILE	74	95	60	64	86	95
COLOMBIA	79	86b	61	68b	83	na
MEXICO	68	62	70d	51	na	na
PERU	47	73c	30	48	51	72
VENEZUELA	60a	89	43d	90	na	84

Sources: United Nations (1987: Tables 42-44), Pan American Health Organization
a 1964 b 1979 c 1983 d 1984

Some cities, of course, were much more effective in improving their services than others and in places infrastructure provision continues to be very poor. In Lima, only 70 per cent of households had a tap inside the home in 1990 and 20 per cent were dependent on public standpipes or water trucks. Worse still was the fact that the pipes did not always contain water: 55 per cent of homes had water for less than 6 hours per day and only 19 per cent for more than 13 hours.

In general, the larger and more affluent cities were able to service their populations more effectively than their smaller and less prosperous cousins. Nevertheless, there were some highly industrialised cities where the local population faired badly; Monterrey, Buenos Aires, São Paulo and Valencia all fell far below the standards of most other cities even in the same country. Only 59 per cent of the population of São Paulo is linked to the sewerage system and only 18 per cent of sewage is treated before it is dumped into the river system. In Lima, 19 per cent of homes have no direct water supply and 11 per cent do not even have water in the building. Among the poorest 30 per cent of homes, the figures are 31 per cent and 21 per cent respectively.

If there are major variations in the quality of service provision

---

CAUSING A STINK IN SÃO PAULO

When an alligator appeared in the Tiete (the main river running through São Paulo) people were more puzzled about how it survived among the sewage than how it got there. In the dry season, 60 per cent of the river's volume is made of domestic and industrial waste. It pours into the river at a rate of 33 cubic metres a second. Industrial waste makes up two thirds of the effluence dumped in the river. The rest is human waste, the result of the government's failure to match the city's growth with sewage treatment facilities.

Jan Rocha, *The Guardian*, 4 October 1991.

---

between cities, the variations between different areas within the same city are sometimes even more marked. The upper and middle-income groups are well serviced while delivery to the less affluent areas of the city is often poor. The differences between income groups is clearly demonstrated in Table 6.2.

The quality of service does not only depend on income, however, but also upon the age of a settlement. While the poor living in older settlements tend to have access to most services, those living in new settlements are

Table 6.2
Service delivery by income group in Lima, 1990
(percent with service)

SERVICE	BOTTOM 10%	TOP 10%	ALL LIMA
WATER IN HOME	57.3	91.3	70.0
WATER TRUCK	20.0	4.4	8.6
13 HOURS OR MORE OF WATER	19.0	23.5	18.6
SEWERAGE	63.5	93.2	71.5
ELECTRIC LIGHT	87.5	98.6	90.5
COOK WITH KEROSENE	87.8	12.8	55.7

Source: Glewwe and Hall (1992:30)

Figure 6.1
Consumption of water in Santiago

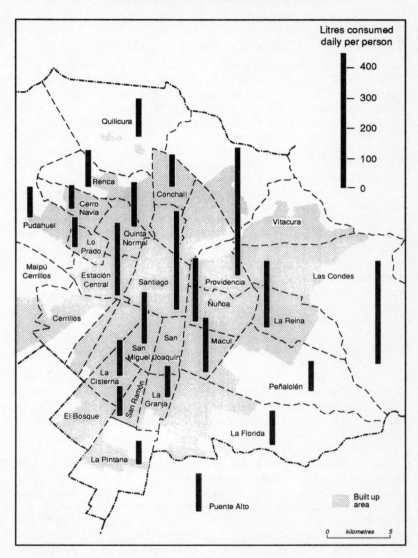

Source: Fuensalida (1987)

often less well provided for. The importance of age can be demonstrated in Figure 6.1 which shows how the consumption of water in Santiago deteriorates with distance from the central area, particularly towards the south and northwest of the city where most of the poor live.

The administration of service delivery

Any improvement in service delivery over the years has come partly from better administration and partly from investing more in infrastructure and maintenance. The quality of administration has been reflected in the changing structure of the utility companies. At the turn of the century, many urban services were operated by private companies, many of them foreign-owned. Before 1930, a Canadian company supplied the electricity and ran the trams in Mexico City, Rio de Janeiro and São Paulo. Private companies provided the first light in Bogotá, Caracas and Lima, and in Argentina and Uruguay, foreign companies built most of the infrastructure.

Elsewhere, municipal enterprises had been set up to improve infrastructure and services. In Medellín, a municipal electricity company was established in 1918; in Bogotá the municipality bought the tram service from an American entrepreneur in 1910. In São Paulo a state enterprise was established to build drains and sewers in 1926. Indeed, as the pace of urban growth accelerated, the state became more and more involved in the provision of services. It took over the less competent private companies and nationalised others. In Argentina, the outflow of foreign capital in the 1930s encouraged the state to take over the running of the railways, telephones and electricity. In Mexico, Lázaro Cárdenas set up a federal electricity agency in 1937 and the private company supplying Mexico City was nationalised in 1960. In Caracas, a private telephone company was nationalised in 1953 and a national water company established in 1943.

Private companies continued to operate in some cities. In 1990, private companies were still providing the electricity in Caracas, Lima, and Valencia, running the buses in Bogotá, Guadalajara, and parts of Lima and Mexico City, and supplying water in Guatemala City and in parts of Santiago.

Whether the services were run publicly or privately, however, there was a transformation in the way companies operated, with the pace of change accelerating after 1950. Many were forced to improve their performance by constant demands for a better service. Sometimes the change came in response to an effective popular protest, sometimes as the result of a disaster or some kind of scandal. Occasionally it was stimulated by the realisation that something simply had to be done to improve the level of services. After a major electricity black-out the government might respond by setting up a commission to investigate the cause and hope that both the

Low-tech water supply in El Agustín, Lima   Daniel Pajuelo/El Agustín/TAFOS

black-out and the commission would soon be forgotten. It might throw money at the problem and let the existing agency step up its investment programme. Once in a while, it would try to restructure the agency, establishing a new institution that might actually work. Gradually, Latin American governments began to recognise that without competent management, urban problems would certainly increase and would spark political unrest.

But the pressure for reform did not originate only from inside the Latin American city. Insofar as governments needed to expand capacity they needed to borrow large sums from national and, increasingly, from foreign banks. Many of these banks refused to lend money unless they were assured that the utilities would be run more efficiently. When the World Bank and the Inter-American Development Bank became major financiers of service improvements the pressure for reform intensified. The loans were available on strict terms; governments could either take the advice of these agencies or refuse the loans.

The general tenor of the advice was that companies should become more technically competent, should be run along more commercial lines, should cut the level of subsidy and, above all, should reduce the degree of political interference. Service agencies should act as autonomous technical bureaucracies, not as pawns in the game of winning votes. They should be judged on their ability to increase service provision, not in terms of whether they gave jobs to the supporters of one party or provided services to a politically favoured settlement.

Many governments in Latin America took this advice, and the loans which went with it. They established large, and sometimes competent, agencies. In Colombia, the bureaucracies which ran electricity, sewerage, telephone and water services in Bogotá, Cali and Medellín represented a vast improvement on what had existed before. In Santiago, despite recent efforts at privatisation, public enterprises have successfully managed the metro and water companies. EMOS, the water company, has succeeded in expanding provision while remaining financially sound.

The efforts to depoliticise service agencies were not always popular. Politicians did not take kindly to losing control over the allocation of jobs in public bureaucracies and services to the slums. How could they win votes if they were unable to get community leaders a job in the electricity agency or to persuade it to provide light in their supporters' neighbourhood? Indeed, in many cities the attempt to establish technical bureaucracies never succeeded. The quality of service delivery in cities such as Lima, Acapulco, Recife and Guayaquil continues to be a disgrace. And even in cities where competent organisations were established, some agencies continued to demonstrate the worst practices of Latin American public administration. In Bogotá, the public bus company regularly lost large sums of money, failed to repair its buses, and employed ten drivers for every bus. There were few complaints when it was wound up some years back.

A second major problem was that the technical bureaucracies sometimes became insensitive to popular demands. They increased tariffs too frequently or they displaced self-help settlements along the route of a new road or service line. This kind of high-handed action was particularly common in countries with military governments. In the late 1970s, for example, the São Paulo Metro Company drove a new railway through a central part of the city, displacing the population with no warning and little compensation. As Richard Batley (1982) shows, faced by the choice of delaying completion of the railway, and therefore suffering from penalty clauses built into a foreign loan, or evicting poor people from their homes, the company chose the latter, much cheaper, option. Nor was the operation of technically competent agencies always very equitable. All too often, technical agencies failed to help the poor. In Brazil, the National Housing Bank was extremely successful in building housing and apartments but much less effective in delivering houses to the poor.[1] Even worse, loans to the middle class were financed by compulsory deductions from working-class incomes.

With the debt crisis and recession of the 1980s, the problems facing such service agencies grew. As local currencies were devalued, the cost of repaying foreign loans escalated. Many companies were forced to raise tariff levels to cover the increasing cost of repayment. Structural adjustment programmes required governments to remove subsidies on service delivery. In Mexico, subsidies on most government services were slashed, falling as a proportion of gross national product from ten per cent in 1980 to four per cent in 1986.

Highly subsidised tariffs gradually gave way to more economic charges. In Mexico City, for example, the cost of travelling on the underground rose from one peso to 50 pesos in December 1987, 100 in December 1988, 300 in November 1990, to 400 pesos in November 1991. Such rapid rises sometimes led to violence. Riots broke out in Caracas in February 1989 when private companies tried to double bus fares and refused to accept student cards (see p.148). In the 1970s, rising fares, combined with the poor service, led to frequent riots on the railways of Rio de Janeiro and São Paulo. Similarly, in Guatemala City, rising bus fares were one of the ingredients leading to widespread looting, riots and strikes in 1985. The question of public service charges is posing a difficult political dilemma in a number of Latin American cities.

In many cities, governments are now offering a different recipe for improvement; privatisation. Many recommend privatisation as the only means by which to cut government expenditure and improve service delivery. Faced by the dilemma of running public companies with large deficits and nothing with which to finance the deficit, the attraction of privatisation is particularly intoxicating. The perceived effectiveness of privatisation in improving public services in Britain and in Chile (whether or not that perception is justified) and the aggressive selling of privatisation by the World Bank and the International Monetary Fund, have had their effect in most Latin American countries. Privatisation is the current flavour of the decade in Argentina, Colombia and Mexico and is threatening to become so elsewhere.

While privatisation is currently very popular and has led to the sale of many state-run airlines, banks and mining companies in Latin America, few public utilities were sold during the 1980s. Only telephone and telecommunications companies have been regularly put up for sale; state companies have been sold, or are being threatened with sale, in Argentina, Chile, Colombia, Mexico, Uruguay and Venezuela, although even this has mainly affected intercity and international telephone services. The rubbish collection services have been contracted out to private operators in Bogotá and in several Venezuelan cities. The electricity generating companies have been sold in Chile, and there are similar plans in Argentina. In the latter, twenty-year concessions are being offered to run the postal services and all water and sanitation companies. The Buenos Aires underground system is also up for sale.

Despite this long list, the bulk of public service agencies have not been sold. Privatisation has been slowed by the difficulty of finding buyers. The only companies able to take over the more significant state corporations are foreign-owned transnationals, and few governments are keen to sell strategic industries to such companies. In the field of urban infrastructure and services there is an additional problem. Not only are most companies unprofitable and weighed down by large debts, but their responsibilities are closely regulated by law. Few private companies are keen to enter into this arena without full autonomy, but equally few governments are willing to let private companies operate free of public scrutiny in such a politically sensitive area. Consequently, there has been little divestiture of public agencies in the urban infrastructure and services fields. Recent announcements in Mexico, Argentina and Venezuela suggest that the pace of change may accelerate.

The only real privatisation that has occurred in the urban services field is that described by Hernando de Soto in his controversial book, *The other path (1989)*. In the absence of an adequate public transport system in Lima, private companies run the taxis and minibuses which move people around the city. Where there are no water pipes, private water tankers move into the self-help settlements. In Buenos Aires, the failure of the public telephone company has led to private initiative decorating office blocks with informal solutions, and in most cities, some low-income settlements are forced to steal their own electricity.

It is clear that if public facilities are unavailable, both rich and poor are prepared to pay for private services. But this is hardly a desirable development. Private companies do supply water to the poor and private buses do get them to work. But the service is rarely adequate and is sometimes dangerous. Of course, any kind of service delivery is undoubtedly better than none, but to approve of informal service delivery seems to be a way of relieving the state of even more of its social responsibilities.

Bumper-to-bumper fumes in Mexico City

Julio Etchart/Reportage

Should we be praising the shift of responsibility from the public to the private sector or urging the state to become more efficient and to generate more resources to do its rightful job?

Transport

In 1940, 48,000 private vehicles were registered in the Federal District of Mexico, in 1980 there were 1.9 million, and currently there are around 3.0 million. There were 3,000 cars in Caracas in 1934 compared to around 600,000 today. While the expansion of motorised transport and particularly the development of public bus systems can bring huge advantages, the emergence of widespread car ownership is more problematic. The car contributes both to air pollution and traffic congestion: 85 per cent of the vehicles circulating in Mexico City are private cars which, with an average occupancy of 1.4 persons, account for only 17 per cent of the total travellers. In 1980, there were so many vehicles in Caracas that they were travelling at an average speed of only 10 kilometres per hour. In Mexico City, the average speed during rush hour is estimated to be only 16 kilometres per hour. Most Latin American cities today suffer from a combination of traffic congestion, air pollution and traffic-related urban blight.

Few governments have been prepared to introduce tough measures

YEARS OF CHAOS: THE BUS SYSTEM OF BOGOTA

There was a public bus company in Bogotá, but it operated very few routes.
It was meant to improve the quality of the bus service, but over the years it
did little to achieve that end. Its main contribution to life in Bogotá was to
have provided jobs for those with political influence. The badly run company
had far too many employees. At one stage of the 1970s it had more buses
rotting in the port of Buenaventura, than were operating on the streets of the
capital; the company could not afford to pay the customs duties!

Today, all of Bogotá's buses are run by private companies, some
supported by a government subsidy. The companies obtain the rights to
operate along particular routes but they do not own most of the buses that
operate under their name; most buses are owned by their drivers, some by
two or three separate individuals.

Fares vary according to the kind of bus: executive buses, which
guarantee a seat, charge 37 US cents, minibuses 27 US cents, and the
ordinary, often desperately crowded, bus only 15 US cents. Otherwise fares
are the same whatever the route and on the cheaper buses whatever the
distance travelled. While this simplifies charging for the driver, it brings
certain difficulties. The main problem is that since routes are not equally
profitable, all of the operators want to run their buses along the same roads
in the city centre. Few of the companies or drivers want to operate in the
poorer parts of the city, especially where the settlements climb up the
mountainside. While most operate some routes to the outer suburbs, nearly
all of the buses sooner or later pass through the centre of the city. Although
private cars were banned from Carrera Décima in 1977, the concentration of
so many buses in one road brings dreadful congestion. At most times of day
it is much quicker to walk along the central kilometre stretch than to sit on a
bus.

Until recently, all bus routes were extensively subsidised. However,
in an attempt to cut its transport budget, the government has been encouraging the development of minibuses which do not receive subsidies. One
consequence is that the number of buses has increased dramatically, the
other that the average number of passengers carried by each bus has fallen
by more than half. The obvious outcome is that congestion has increased.

Congestion is also made worse by the nature of the fare system.
Drivers are paid a minimal basic salary and most of their income depends
upon the number of passengers they carry. Every driver, therefore, is
competing for passengers. There are bus stops in Bogotá but, with the
exception of a couple of heavily policed streets, they are ignored. In an
attempt to increase the number of passengers, drivers stop frequently and

swing across lanes when they spot a passenger. It is estimated that they stop four times every kilometre. The quality of driving is also affected by the drivers' long working day - frequently from 5.30 am to 8.00 pm so that both rush hours can be fitted in.

Recently, serious efforts have been made to improve the system. A major arterial route has been adapted so that four lanes are reserved for buses and so that passengers can only be picked up and let off at regularly placed 'stations'. The ordinary bus stop limits the number of passengers who can be let on and off; the station can channel passengers on the platforms in a more ordered way and can increase the number of travellers. The system was first developed in Curitiba in Brazil where it proved highly successful in cutting average journey times and increasing the number of passengers carried. If it proves effective in Bogotá, it will work anywhere!

Source: Acevedo (1990) and Cifuentes (c1979).

to deal with these problems. The most common response has been to limit car use during the working week. One-fifth of private cars in Mexico City and Santiago have been banned from the streets on each working day, and a similar scheme was introduced, and abandoned, in Caracas. While this measure has had some positive effects, it has not cut congestion greatly because some households buy a second car and most drivers simply postpone their shopping or leisure trips to another day when they are permitted to drive. Certainly, official Mexican claims that during the first two months of the 'no driving today' programme petrol consumption in Mexico City fell by 11 per cent are difficult to believe. In any case, consumption rose during 1990 by 7 per cent. In Santiago, official sources claim that the policy cuts traffic flows by ten per cent.

Without severe controls on private car use, the effectiveness of the public bus system is severely reduced. Few cities have special lanes for buses and segregated bus lanes such as those initiated in Curitiba, and which are now being implemented along one major road in Bogotá, are few and far between. In the meantime, most passengers suffer from bus journeys which are both slow and uncomfortable. They can also be dangerous. Buses in Bogotá have long been notorious for pickpockets, and Paulo Câmara's recent survey in Rio de Janeiro suggests that the situation there is far worse: 17 per cent of passengers had been robbed or assaulted, 18 per cent had seen others assaulted and a further 6 per cent fell into both categories. Nor were the bus drivers in Rio very safe, with 20-25 raids being made on fare boxes every day during 1989.

The Caracas metro author's photo

In an attempt to improve the transport system in Santiago, the military government encouraged new companies to operate bus routes. From 1983 fares were freed from restriction and the number of buses operating increased dramatically. Between 1977 and 1989, the number of buses roughly doubled and the number of taxibuses increased roughly two-and-a-half times. Unfortunately, bus fares rose by 150 per cent during the same period and between 1982 and 1988, the average cost of travel is estimated to have risen from 9 per cent of the monthly minimum wage to 21 per cent. Higher fares and larger numbers of buses have led to the whole transport system being underutilised. Too many people cannot afford to travel, a fact amply illustrated by the rise in the proportion of journeys on foot, from 17 per cent in 1977 to 31 per cent in 1989.

A similar effect is likely in Bogotá where subsidies have been reduced substantially and fares have risen in real terms. In May 1992, the cheapest bus journey cost 95 pesos. Assuming that only one bus was necessary to get to work, then the daily return journey would cost 9 per cent of the daily minimum wage. Changing buses each way, of course, would double the cost to a wholly unaffordable level. Since these buses are extremely crowded and uncomfortable, transportation for the poor is becoming a major problem .

Many would argue, of course, that the only solution to the transport problems of the major cities is to build a metro system. This is precisely what governments have done in seven major cities of the region. Although the underground railway in Buenos Aires was opened in 1913, the other six systems are all quite recent. The first of the modern lines was inaugurated in Mexico City in 1969, followed by new lines in São Paulo and Santiago in 1974 and in Rio de Janeiro in 1979, in Caracas in 1983. Major new systems are being built in Brasília, Lima and Medellín.[2]

Most of the operating systems have been extended over the years and new lines are under construction in Caracas and Mexico City . Mexico City has by far the longest network, totalling 141 kilometres; the next longest system is that of Buenos Aires, with 35 kilometres. The rest are hardly networks at all, for the undergrounds in Caracas, Rio de Janeiro, Santiago and São Paulo have only two lines. Even in Mexico City, the current network of eight lines covers only a small part of the vast urban area. While there are plans to expand the system into the State of Mexico, the current system is confined to the Federal District (Figure 6.2). Vast numbers of people have to travel on buses and *camionetas* to get to the metro station.

Even though the metro in Mexico City only accounts for 15 per cent of the capital's passenger journeys, it still carried 4.1 million passengers per day in 1987 - a statistic that anyone trapped on the system during rush hour would accept without question! The metro systems also tend to be fairly well run. According to Oscar Figueroa and Etienne Henry (1988:8), "In most cases they exhibit a quality of service and level of organisation that is difficult to find anywhere else in the city; to enter the metro in these cities is to bury oneself in a world cut off from the daily pattern of urban underdevelopment."

Given the seeming effectiveness of the metros, many argue that the systems should be extended and that new metros should be built in other Latin American cities. However, there is a fundamental problem in that building metro systems, particularly underground lines, is inordinately expensive. Many cities have looked at the option only to decide reluctantly that they can simply not afford it. The only new systems currently under development are in Brasília and Medellín. Building the metro in Medellín has caused a major financial crisis, and with the Colombian government refusing to bail out the city, there are considerable doubts about whether it can be finished. In the context of economic recession, and given existing levels of external debt, new metro systems are a luxury which few cities can afford.

Even the existing systems face problems. In Mexico City, where there are plans for a major expansion, many lines work below their full capacity. Neither the Caracas nor the Santiago systems have enough passengers. In Buenos Aires, age is taking its toll and underinvestment has led to a deteriorating service. Similarly, the metro in Rio de Janeiro faces an acute financial

Figure 6.2
Mexico City: a metro for some

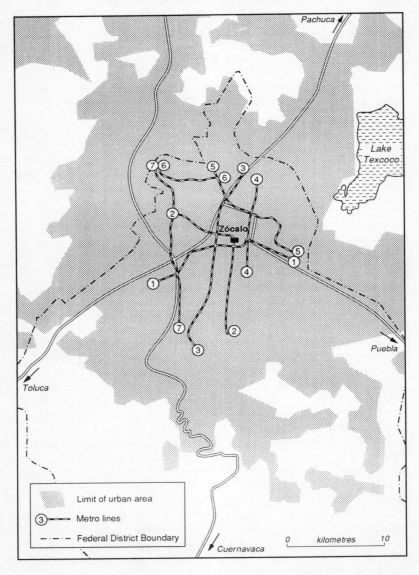

problem which has severely reduced its effectiveness. Levels of maintenance are inadequate and, because fares are higher than on the bus, the number of passengers using the system is falling. In 1990, it was carrying only 245,000 passengers per day, mostly between the wealthier parts of the city.

Pollution and the environment

It is claimed that two million people in Mexico City are suffering from diseases caused or aggravated by air pollution. On 17 March 1992, all Mexico City school children under 14 years of age were ordered to stay at home because air pollution had reached a record high of 398 microgrammes of suspended particles per cubic metre. The following week, the mayor of Mexico City declared a 28-day state of environmental emergency due to the continuing high levels of pollution.

Mexico City's air has long been very unhealthy. Temperature inversions and the high altitude certainly aggravate the situation but the direct cause is the combination of poor management and unregulated economic growth. The deforestation and erosion of the land around the city creates dust which is whipped up by winds during the dry season. In addition, the three million road vehicles generate 5.2 million tons of contaminants which contribute around 40 per cent of the city's pollution.

IMPROVING THE ENVIRONMENT: RECENT EFFORTS IN MEXICO CITY

Mexico City's air has been awful for years. Despite widespread complaints, governments did little to rectify the problems. Only when Carlos Salinas de Gortari came to power in 1988 was action taken. In October 1990, his government announced the introduction of a US$2.5 billion programme, a figure which has since been revised upwards to US$4.6 billion. Action was taken for a variety of reasons. First, pollution levels had reached extreme levels and the authorities were forced to close schools in 1992 because of the state of the atmosphere. Second, the government, which was badly beaten in the national capital in the 1988 elections, believed that environmental measures could be a vote winner. Although jobs would be lost and taxes would have to be raised, removing the worst air polluters and introducing better sanitation systems would be popular. Third, the government was committed to joining the North American Free Trade Agreement. One of the barriers to the signing of such an agreement in the United States is the fear that a lack of environmental controls in Mexico will lead to American companies moving south to escape the more severe controls in the north. As a result, the Salinas administration needs to demonstrate that it is being tough on the polluters.

In November 1989, the government introduced a policy, which had previously been practised in Caracas and Santiago, to control car use in Mexico City. Every private car was prohibited from using the roads one day per week. The limited effect of this control is demonstrated by the fact that petrol consumption in the capital increased 18 per cent between 1988 and 1991 (*The Economist*, 4 April 1992).

In 1990, it was agreed that all buses and taxis would be gradually replaced by vehicles with catalytic converters running on unleaded petrol. In December 1991, the government ordered that all taxis built before 1984 (about half the city's total of 52,000) should be replaced. In March 1991 the PEMEX oil refinery in Mexico City was also closed with the loss of some 5,400 jobs. Without warning, and seemingly on the direct orders of the president, the flow of crude to the refinery was shut off. Neither the management nor the workers had been informed. There was no protest because trade union leaders believed that the closure would be extremely popular with the average citizen. Certainly the plant was a major polluter, spewing 53,000 tons of carbon monoxide, 15,000 tons of sulphur dioxide and 3,000 tons of nitrogen oxide into the air every year and contributing an estimated 4 per cent of all Mexico City's 4.3 million tons of contaminents. In addition, it was also a constant source of danger for the population living around the plant. When it was built in the 1930s, it was distant from the built-up area, but today it is surrounded by housing. Local people described it as a time bomb waiting to go off; the badly maintained plant would sooner or later have caused a major disaster.

In addition to closing the refinery, some 600 plants were temporarily or permanently closed in Mexico City during 1991 because they failed to comply with the government's emission standards. In order to re-open they had to deposit a bank bond equal to the cost of emission control equipment. In March 1992, 250 industries were instructed to cut their production by between half and three-quarters due to the state of the atmosphere. In addition to controls, the government offered credit facilities to Mexico City's 32,000 industrial companies to install equipment to control emissions.

The campaign against air pollution included measures to improve fuel quality, restructure public transportation, modernise industrial production, install vehicle emission control systems, plant trees in the city and restore the environmental quality of surrounding rural areas. A US$100 million loan from the InterAmerican Development Bank is being used to support the programme. Mexico is using the loan to buy back its foreign debt on the secondary market. The proceeds from this debt-for-nature buyback will reduce Mexico's foreign debt by about US$21 million. The money saved will be used to build environmental promotion centres and to support environmental measures in the rural zone surrounding the metropolitan area.

Another 30 per cent is pumped into the air by the city's industries. The rest is mainly due to the lack of adequate garbage and sewerage systems, and rotting waste and excrement add greatly to the city's atmospheric problems. Only in the last three years have serious efforts been made to remedy the situation.

Air pollution produces particularly unpleasant living environments in industrial areas where there is often little control over the waste emitted by large manufacturing companies. In the early 1980s, for example, terrible problems had developed in the Brazilian city of Cubatão, where two dozen major companies had set up factories. Most of these plants were heavy polluters and, in 1984, it was estimated that they released more than 200 tons of particles into the atmosphere every day. With the city lying in at the foot of a range of mountains, it was particularly prone to temperature inversions which made it difficult for the pollution to escape. The fumes from the steel, fertiliser, cement and petrochemical plants produced a noxious brew which hung over the city and its 100,000 inhabitants. In September 1984, air conditions were so bad that the governor declared a state of emergency and ordered part of the city to be evacuated.

Fortunately, the events of 1984 led to the introduction of a major clean-up campaign in Cubatão which cut the emission of particles by 87 per cent in four years. The need to control pollution levels, however, does not seem to have been learned in most Latin American cities. In Caracas, for example, recurrent efforts to move the La Vega cement plant have left some 300,000 people under constant bombardment from the factory chimneys.

Pollution levels continue to be a major problem in most of the region's largest cities. The Metropolitan Region of Santiago is rapidly becoming one of the most highly polluted urban areas in the world. There has long been a heavy layer of smog hanging over the city but the situation has clearly deteriorated in recent years. Walking around the central areas of the city is now extremely unpleasant. There is no escape even in one of the city's major parks, the Quinta Normal, where the pollution is visibly affecting the growth of the trees.

The topography and climate of Santiago favour the accumulation of polluting particles and gases over the city, particularly during the winter months. Recent increases in vehicle emissions have led to a deterioration in air quality and a build-up in the concentration of toxic elements in the atmosphere. During the winter of 1989, levels of carbon monoxide concentration were three times as high as recommended by international environmental standards, while those of respirable particles were over nine times higher.

It is not just the air that is polluted. Some 300 million cubic metres of untreated sewage is pumped into the two rivers of the city and its main canal. Even in more affluent parts of the city, such as Providencia, the smell

POWER TO THE POLLUTERS: THE LA VEGA CEMENT PLANT IN
CARACAS

The La Vega cement plant occupies a site in the southwest of Caracas.
Founded in the first decade of the century, it is now in the middle of a
densely populated residential area. Some 300,000 people live in settlements
affected by pollution from the La Vega plant. It is claimed that respiratory
diseases are very much higher in La Vega and Montalbán than in the rest of
Caracas, and that local children suffer from very high rates of bronchitis.
This realisation led to the population protesting against the continued
presence of La Vega and two other major polluters, a steel plant (Siderúrgica
Venezolana) and a synthetic flooring plant (Suelatex).
    In January 1975, a presidential decree ordered contaminating
industry in Caracas to leave the city. In 1976 another decree established
precisely which industries were required to leave within five years. If they
had not left by that time, they would be forced to close. In 1981, when
nothing had actually happened, the local community began to organise
protests against the continued presence of the plant. In August, the Ministry
of Development gave the company one year to move the plant, a decision
ratified by the Cabinet.
    The company did not wish to leave because of the high costs that
relocation would involve. Since the buildings and infrastructure accounted for
half the total investment in the plant it would be enormously expensive to
move. In 1981, the company estimated that the total investment required for
a new plant would be around US$2 million. In addition, the factory supplied
90 per cent of Caracas's cement, and relocation would raise the cost of
supplying the capital. The plant also employed 1,000 workers, most of whom
would lose their jobs if the plant moved. In any case, the company claimed
that it had modern electric filters on all its chimneys and that no-one could
demonstrate that the pollution came from the La Vega plant.
    In 1981, the company appealed to the Supreme Court of Justice
about the legality of the decree and requested one year's postponement on
its departure while the Court made up its mind. The Court decided in the
company's favour on the grounds that government officials had done too
little to encourage the company to move and because it was impossible for a
plant of that size to move in a period of one year. It postponed any move
until the constitutional legality of the original decree of 1975 could be
determined.
    The original decree had been approved by a president who was a
member of the Democratic Action party. In 1981, during the celebrations for
the 400 year anniversary of the foundation of the the the Parish of La Vega,

President Luis Herrera Campíns of the rival COPEI party promised that the cement plant would be forced to leave. The fact that the plant could escape the resolutions of presidents from both major political parties is remarkable. Even more remarkable were the grounds for further postponement; the company did not have to move because it could not be expected to move within one year. If the original decree had been produced in 1981, the decision would have been thoroughly reasonable. But, it was not. The original decision was taken in 1975 and the company was given five years to comply! Subsequently, the Court decided that the original decree was not constitutional. As such, the cement company can continue to pollute this area of Caracas.

from the river is unpleasant.

The effects of this pollution on health are very worrying; the city has a particularly high rate of typhoid largely due to the widespread practice of using untreated water to irrigate crops. Air pollution is also taking its toll; in 1988, 300,000 additional cases of broncopulmonary diseases were recorded in Santiago. Only in 1990 did the government announce serious measures to tackle the problems, and in April 1993 it reintroduced controls over car use.

Disasters

Latin America's cities are subject to several kinds of 'natural' disaster: floods, hurricanes, earthquakes and volcanic eruptions. The whole of the mountain chain which runs from Mexico down through Central America and along the Pacific Coast of South America to Tierra del Fuego is susceptible to earthquakes and volcanic eruptions. Earthquakes have repeatedly hit Guatemala City and San Salvador, devastated Managua in 1972, destroyed much of Popayán in 1983, and hit both Mexico City and Santiago very badly in 1985. In recent years, volcanic eruptions destroyed Armero in 1985 and another Colombian city, Pasto, is in some danger from the newly active Galeras volcano.

Elsewhere, floods and landslides are a recurrent problem. In the Chilean port of Antofagasta, more than one hundred people died and 700 were injured in 1991, when torrential rain caused landslides. In Caracas, Manizales (Colombia) and Rio de Janeiro, landslides are a more common event, regularly threatening self-help settlements located on the mountain slopes. In August 1993 more than 150 people were killed and thousands left homeless when Tropical Storm Bret caused a massive landslide on a hillside Caracas shanty town.

Of course, natural events such as storms and earthquakes only become disasters when they hit built-up areas. Even then, their effect depends less on the intensity of the storm or earthquake than on how the city has been constructed. This was demonstrated all too clearly by the earthquake in Mexico City where despite the terrible damage in the central areas, many buildings were not affected. Within the affected zone, it was buildings of a particular age and height that suffered the most severe damage. It is widely believed that the large number of public buildings that were destroyed was a result of the corruption and incompetence that was associated with their construction. While little can be done to prevent natural hazards, their effect can be substantially reduced by building to a certain standard of construction. Unfortunately, Latin American cities are not always built with such hazards in mind.

If few 'natural' disasters are wholly natural, too many disasters have been brought about entirely by human folly. During the last ten years, for example, hundreds of people have been killed by industrial accidents in Cubatão, Guadalajara and Mexico City. In Cubatão, a leaking pipe line in February 1984 led to an explosion which killed more than 500 people living in a shanty town along its route. In Mexico City, an explosion in the state-owned liquid gas storage plant in the suburb of San Juan Ixhuatepec in November 1984 caused the deaths of at least 500 people and perhaps as many as 1,500. In both Cubatão and Mexico City, the effects of the explosions were worsened by the fact that low-income housing had filled in the gap that had originally been left between the facility and the nearest settlement.

PEMEX, the Mexican state oil company was also responsible for the explosion in Guadalajara in April 1992. Not only did the explosion kill at least 200 people, and possibly as many as one thousand, but an area of 26 blocks in the central area of the city was devastated. Some 2,000 homes, 1,400 businesses and 600 vehicles were destroyed or severely damaged. The explosion was eventually blamed on a leak of petrol from a pipeline into the city's sewerage system.

Notes

(1) For discussions of this interesting case, see Klak (1990), Sachs (1990) and Shidlo (1990)

(2) What precisely constitutes a metro is debateable. As such certain other rail systems in Latin America should be mentioned. In Brazil, modernised urban rail systems were opened in Belo Horizonte, Porto Alegre and Recife during the 1980s, although none operate underground. In Mexico, both Guadalajara and Monterrey have recently opened light rail systems which have short underground sections. The Medellín system is certainly a metro but operates on raised track rather than underground.

Further Reading

Useful sources on service provision in different Latin American cities include Austin and Lewis (1970), Balderas and Molero (1988), Chang (1969), Dupuy (1987), Genatios (1969), Vargas and Zambrano (1988), Webb and Fernández (1991) and Zatz (1991). Various figures from these sources have been included in the text.

Useful sources on urban transportation include Câmara (1991), Figueroa (1990), Figueroa and Henry (1988), Lizt Mendoza (1988), Molinero (1991), Morales (1988) and Ovalles and Córdoba (1986). Most of the figures cited in this chapter are drawn from these sources.

Interesting discussions of urban pollution include World Bank (1992b) and Hardoy, Mitlin and Satterthwaite (1992).

Accounts of disasters in Latin America include Walker (1991).

7

URBAN PROTEST

"As though the entire valley had been soaked with gasoline, the violence spread through the Caracas valley and then up the mountainsides into the *barrios*. Streets were barricaded; buses, automobiles, and vans were burned; stores were looted. As the news spread, nineteen other cities exploded" (Hellinger, 1991:192).

A fairly ordinary day in Latin America? Certainly much of what appears in European and North American newspapers about the region would encourage such a view. We tend to hear much about spectacular outbreaks of unrest and violence: the most recent military coup, bombs planted by a revolutionary political group, the killing of strikers by the army or the police. And yet the reality is rather different. There are, of course, more violent episodes than in the cities of developed countries, but not all that many more. Protests do spill onto the streets, some demonstrators do get killed and injured. But the very fact that demonstrations actually hit the headlines means that they are not all that common, let alone bombs, riots or guerrilla attacks. Any violence in Latin American streets is much more likely to be an ordinary criminal act than anything remotely to do with politics.

Of course, it would be absurd to say that ordinary Latin Americans never protest. Protest marches often head for the central square, strikes paralyse major factories and offices, people invade land, and community groups frequently visit government offices to demand better services. Sometimes office windows are broken, buses are burned, supermarkets looted and roads blocked. In poor societies, some degree of violence is almost inevitable because people face daily deprivation and frustration. The rate of inflation is often far too high, and incomes are usually far too low; too many people live in housing without adequate services, and government is too often inept. Politics also directly affects people's lives, not only determining the government of the day but also which set of supporters will occupy government posts.

But how much social protest is there in the Latin American city? Here we face a problem. According to the authorities in some countries, there is none at all. Governments do not like to admit that there are street protests, let alone deaths and injuries, since it is not good for their image and deters tourists. In some countries the press, radio and television are controlled by the authorities, and there is little media coverage of social conflict. On the other hand, according to some academic studies, Latin America seems to be constantly seething with protest, to be full of revolutionary movements. In short, how much protest there is depends largely on what you read.

My own view is that there is relatively little protest given the appalling conditions in which so many people live. What constantly surprises me in Latin America is how long-suffering most people actually are. The poor tolerate overcrowded buses, inefficient bureaucracies, inadequate services, low pay, and official corruption with a patience that would do credit to Job. For someone coming from a developed country, it is incomprehensible why the poor of Latin America protest as little as they do.

This chapter attempts to examine whether this relative passivity is a consistent feature of the region's urban life. Why are the events in Caracas, described at the beginning of the chapter, not an everyday occurrence? Why do Latin Americans put up with as much as they do? At the same time, I do not want to give the impression that everything is peaceful and everyone passive. Organised protests and occasional outbreaks of violence do take place and I will attempt to explain the triggers that occasionally lead to social unrest. Why did the riots break out in Caracas in 1989, why did the citizens of Mexico City protest after the earthquake in 1985, why did the people of Monterrey invade land and take on the police throughout the 1970s? To what extent is it possible to give a general explanation of these occurrences? How far do explanations linked to terms such as 'urban social movements' and the 'austerity riots' actually take us?

Why is there so little protest?

By protest, I mean conflict which takes place in public places: marches, demonstrations, strikes, riots and outright urban insurgency - the possible aftermath of failed negotiations or when negotiations have never taken place, when 'debate' moves onto the streets. The reason why such conflict is not an everyday phenomenon in most cities can be summarised under four main headings: community attitudes, clientilism, leadership and cooptation and repression.

(1) Community attitudes

One explanation why the urban population does not often riot or protest is that the majority of Latin Americans are politically conservative. As the

THE COLONIA ASKS FOR HELP

"The delegation of petitioners from Colonia X has been waiting patiently for
several hours - seven entire families, including restless children and family
heads who have taken time off from their jobs, led by officers of the
colonia's improvement association. The anteroom leading to the office of a
Federal District functionary is crowded with dozens of similar delegations
from other neighborhoods of the city. The people from Colonia X are urban
squatters, and when finally granted admittance they present a laboriosly
typed petition requesting government recognition of their land tenure rights,
signed by virtually all residents of their community. A spokesman for the
group argues that land titles are essential to assuring a modest inheritance
for their children. Moreover, he continues, security of tenure will stimulate
investment in the construction of permanent houses and commercial
enterprises within the community. The spokesman also observes pointedly
that with property titles residents of the colonia may begin contributing to
government tax revenues. To strengthen the image of their community as
one deserving of government aid, other members of the delegation cite
examples of the hardships they themselves have endured in settling the
land and the efforts they have made to improve the community. They stress
their belief in the government's commitment to humanitarian concerns,
which should ensure that their request will be granted in the interests of
social justice. The office promises that the colonia's situation will be
thoroughly investigated. The session is concluded amid fervent expressions
of the petitioners' support for the incumbent administration."

Source: Cornelius (1975:166)

sociológist Aléjandro Portes (1972:282) puts it: "Few theories have been
more widely held than that of slum radicalism. Few have met with more
consistent rejection from empirical research. Studies in almost every Latin
American capital have found leftist extremism to be weak, or even nonex-
istent, in peripheral slums." Not only that, ordinary Latin Americans are
reluctant to resort to violence. Most regard street protests in a disapproving
light as something that less respectable members of society engage in. It
follows that only quite extraordinary circumstances lead to mass mobilisa-
tion and protest. Wayne Cornelius (1975:167) observed on the basis of his
work in Mexico City that "particularly among low-income city dwellers in
Latin America, demand articulation usually does not involve table-pound-
ing, protest demonstrations, or other aggressive behavior."

Such conservative attitudes are compounded by the day-to-day nature of urban life. Getting involved in politics takes time, and time is at a premium. Not only do people work long days, but many are also busy at the weekends building their homes. They tend to have large families, both nuclear and extended, and families also take time. As Scott Mainwaring (1989:183) observes, the majority of the population of the Baixada Fluminense (in Rio de Janeiro) have difficult lives:

> When they can get jobs, men work long hours for low pay and frequently travel as many as four hours per day to and from work. Women take care of the home and the children, and generally work at least part time as well. The exhausting nature of daily life by itself represents an obstacle to popular participation; people do not find the time or energy to add more commitment to their already difficult lives. In the limited spare time they have, poor people typically focus on a range of issues that have little to do with politics: family life, sports, relaxing.

Perhaps as a result, levels of political participation in most low-income neighbourhoods are relatively low. In Nova Iguaçu, a community in Rio which was active in social protests during the 1970s and 1980s, Mainwaring concludes that no more than 3 per cent of the population had ever been involved. In the late 1960s, participation in the community politics of the consolidated settlements of Lima seldom averaged 10 per cent and was only 6 per cent in Santiago (Portes, 1972:275). In two invasion settlements in Valencia, only one in five families had ever participated in the activities of the residents' associations and four out of five settlements in Mexico City had rates of non-participation ranging from 66 to 82 per cent (Gilbert and Ward, 1985:204). Most surveys have recorded similar kinds of figures.

Of course, there are times when people do participate more actively; they certainly attend community meetings and help petition the authorities during the early stages of settlement formation, and they are particularly active when there is any threat to the settlement. They get involved in demands for basic infrastructure such as electricity and water and also react to emergencies caused by fire, flood, landslides and hurricanes. In these circumstances most families realise that their best interests are served by working together. Yet later, the common interest is much less obvious. As settlements develop they become less homogenous. Longer established households start renting out accommodation, and new tenant families see less purpose in getting involved in community affairs. What is the point of working to get the road paved if you are a tenant? You might not be there next year and in any case better transport might lead to higher rents. Other kinds of division may develop. Political parties may be competing vigorously within the community. I remember talking to one family in Valencia

Local politician presents cooker
to *barrio* organisation, Lima

Maria Teresa de la Cruz/
Ribera del Rio/TAFOS

who were refusing to cooperate with the neighbourhood association: "For five years the new leaders refused to help us run the community, now it is our time to cross our arms while they get on with it."

Not only social divisions but the whole pattern of life can discourage collective action. Once the basics of land and services have been obtained, settlers want to improve their homes and bring up their families as decently as possible. The pressures and responsibilities of home and family tend to lessen urban militancy. Manuel Castells (1983:203) describes attitudes in one of the most politically active and radical settlements in Santiago. Despite their political commitment, "the real dream of most *pobladores* was that Nueva La Habana would one day cease to be a *campamento* and become an average working class *población*." The urban poor generally adopt a strategy of working hard and keeping out of trouble.

At the same time, too much should not be made of the apparently depoliticised side of Latin America's urban poor. Working-class people may be reluctant to protest in the streets or even to organise petitions for the very good reason that they do not believe that this is an effective strategy. The majority have been convinced by governments that negotiation is a more effective policy than confrontation. Through a combination of carrots and, not infrequently, big sticks most Latin American governments have dissuaded people from engaging in open protest.

(2) Clientelism

One of the most effective ways in which Latin American governments have managed to dampen political protest is through clientelism. Politicians and government officials have sought votes and understanding by offering rewards to the community. They have done so on the clear understanding that land, schools or infrastructure are conditional on the neighbourhood's political support.

In addition, the authorities have tried to show that they are always ready to listen to the people. They have encouraged neighbourhood associations and established government offices to communicate and negotiate with those associations. Community Action Councils in Colombia, Societies of Friends of the Bairro in Brazil, Associations of Neighbours in Venezuela and their like have appeared throughout Latin America. The rhetoric has been both sympathetic and populist. At times, they have even provided enough help to convince the population that such associations are worth something. They have built community halls, provided water standpipes, or laid on bus services.

All too often, of course, the flow of services has been little more than a trickle. Apathy has ensued as people realised that there was little point in attending community meetings or listening to visiting politicians. As one Brazilian *favela* dweller said: "The Society of Friends of the Bairro is an organization of directors, and the people never participate in it. To this day, I've never seen those people do anything for the neighbourhood. They only use it during election time. The politicians come in here and ask for votes while making promises they never keep" (Singer, 1982:289). Similar sentiments are easy to come across in Bogotá or Valencia. "You see the politicians two weeks before the election and then they disappear until the next one."

Disillusioned or not, many people continue to hope that things will change and the state will provide services and infrastructure, perhaps because they do not have a great deal of choice. As Robert Gay (1990:664) puts it: "Devoid of economic resources and of the political power necessary to obtain them, clientelist politics has offered and continues to offer the urban poor... a rare opportunity for material gain." And, to an extent they are right. For, as I showed in the last chapter, the quality of services and infrastructure generally improved between 1950 and 1980 in most Latin American cities. Political leaders used this resource to help their clienteles in the *barrios*.

(3) Leadership and co-optation

According to Wayne Cornelius (1975:164-5): "The evidence from Mexico City suggests that strong leadership - whether provided by a *cacique* or by some other type of local leader - can significantly increase the capacity of a low-income community to manipulate the political system in order to secure assistance in community development." The effective leader can obtain resources from political patrons in ways closed to most others. Since resources are limited, what one settlement obtains may no longer be available to another.

PORTRAIT OF A COMMUNITY LEADER IN BOGOTA

Angel María López was the leader of a small settlement in Soacha, a rapidly growing industrial town on the edge of Bogotá. He had lived in the illegal subdivision for fifteen years, indeed ever since it had been founded. He was middle-aged, had five children and lived comfortably, if in no sense ostentatiously.

He owned a small cafe-cum-bar in the settlement and also ran the local outlet of the state-owned (IDEMA) food distribution system. He was also in charge of the distribution of kerosene in the barrio as well as running the main IDEMA store in the centre of town. His control of the IDEMA stores and the kerosene distribution gave him considerable influence over his neighbours because all the products sold through these outlets were subsidised.

He had been an officer in the community association for a number of years before becoming the president of the junta. His influence on the community was strong and he was, by his own admission, tough with the inhabitants. He certainly insisted that all owner-occupiers joined the Community Action association. If he needed to convince them of the benefits of membership, then he might mention that he would not sell kerosene to non-members. He was certainly not universally popular and claimed to have been attacked one night in the barrio by two men.

He had developed considerable political clout in Soacha, indeed, the location of the IDEMA store in the barrio was his doing. He was a deputy councillor having become affiliated to the majority faction of the Liberal Party which now dominated politics in the town. His recruitment from another party occurred after he was arrested for some unspecified misdemeanor when the local political boss happened to be in the police station. The latter, who later became head of the Council, defended his character even though López was his opponent. Whatever the truth behind this strange event, a political deal was struck. López' position on the Council gave him a lot of power with which to obtain financial support for his settlement. If he was tough with his neighbours, then it was also clear that they benefited as a community from his political contacts. He had obtained many facilities for the settlement which were absent from other parts of town.

Angel María López was the closest embodiment to a local *cacique* that I have ever met in Bogotá and his fears for his own safety were clearly not unjustified. Two years after he was first interviewed he was killed. It was never clear who killed him.

Of course, some leaders are effective in obtaining resources for the community. Others are ill-equipped for the job, while some retain their position as leaders precisely because they fail to deliver services. The last kind of leader has been co-opted by the authorities who have given promises of personal favours in return for political peace in the community. Leaders may be offered a job in the bureaucracy, or may gain political advancement, or may benefit from an official blind eye being turned to illegal money-making practices. The leader is happy and so are the authorities, only the community loses out.

Social scientists are divided over the role and effect of cooptation. Susan Eckstein (1977:101), for instance, takes a highly negative view of the process. "Co-optation of leaders and incorporation of local groups has served to establish and reinforce the status quo." She is certainly in the majority, for few writers view such practices positively. However, Scott Mainwaring (1989:188) takes issue with this interpretation. "Most discussions of the cooptation of social movements have been somewhat simplistic; they have almost universally treated cooptation as an evil that social movements must avoid, while its opposite (autonomy) is a goal they must strive for." This view, he believes, is too simple because it ignores the benefits the community obtains. "The possibility of cooptation implies an exchange between the State and a popular movement or leader. The State can coopt only if it provides some resources in return."

(4) Repression

When persuasion, clientelism, cooptation, populist rhetoric and even the occasional carrot fail, there is always the stick. Few Latin American governments deal gently with political protest. Protestors may not be punished during the build-up to an election and they may even win special concessions from populist mayors and governors. However, few governments are indefinitely populist and, during the 1970s, when most governments were unelected and when political repression took a particularly virulent form, heavy-handed tactics were widely used.[1] Both military and non-military regimes frequently resorted to imprisonment, torture and political assassinations. Community leaders were locked up and sometimes killed. Death squads operated with tacit official backing.

Such tactics devastated any kind of political autonomy, even in places where it was relatively well established. In the Novo Iguaçu area of Rio de Janeiro, Mainwaring (1989:171) comments that:

The coup wiped out the most important popular movements. Key leaders of the neighborhood movement were imprisoned, and the repression prevented efforts to coordinate the movement between different neighborhoods. The associations and commissions that survived articulated their demands individually, and there was little public sensitivity to them. The repression and the weakness of local opposition forces made any popular organizing outside the Church almost impossible.

Repression carried on until 1983 and even after. Similar forms of violence were used not just in Brazil but also in Argentina, Chile, Colombia, Peru and Uruguay. The effect on popular protest can be imagined. It is not surprising that there were few street demonstrations; what is surprising is that there were any at all.

In places, of course, community protests were sustained despite highly repressive government tactics. In Santiago, for example, there was a storm of street protests in May 1983 despite ten years of violent repression. But as Schneider (1991:92) admits, the military regime had been badly weakened in 1982 by scandals over how it had mismanaged the economy. And, even if the protests between 1983 and 1986 were widespread, less than one in five settlements was involved. Even then, most of activism was concentrated in settlements which had been founded by the Chilean Communist Party and which had managed to maintain its organisation despite military repression.

By the 1970s, most observers had become extremely pessimistic about the role of grassroots pressure in helping to change the Latin American political system. According to Wayne Cornelius (1975:200):

Rural-urban migration has undoubtedly increased the number of demands made on governments in Mexico and other Latin American countries. But apocalyptic visions of mushrooming popular demands that might overwhelm local or national political systems and generate pressure for major shifts in resource allocation are clearly premature, if not altogether unfounded. Most of the demands on government stemming from the large-scale redistribution of population from rural to urban areas are, regrettably, those that are least likely to threaten the highly inequitable distribution of power and privilege in Mexican society.

Political interest in low-income settlements had been stimulated originally by a general disappointment with the failure of the trades unions and the industrial labour force to fight for social and economic change, and as van Garderen (1989:27) puts it: "..in the early 1970s Marxists lost faith in the labor-proletariat as a vanguard of social change." The discovery that people living in squatter settlements "were more interested in concrete improvements in the day-to-day life than in overall social or political change" was a double blow.

Urban social movements

In 1972, Manuel Castells' book, *The urban question,* presented a new theory of urban radicalism. Originally published in France and clearly influenced by the events of 1968, it was welcomed because it opened up new horizons for Latin American radicalism. Castells' basic argument was that as urbanisation proceeded and urban life became more complicated, large-scale public involvement was required to satisfy the basic needs of the population. The state would be forced to manage what he called the "collective means of production". It would either have to invest itself in housing, infrastructure and public services or persuade the private sector to do so. In intervening in this way, the state would inevitably generate political debate. And, as the difficulties of supplying these services increased - an inevitability given the pace of urban growth and the poverty of the population - arbitration would become very difficult. Eventually, the state would be unable to control political demands and urban protest would break out. If carefully channelled, these protests might develop into true social movements which would demand the radical restructuring of society.

The political Left seized upon this diagnosis and the search for urban social movements was underway. But what most searchers found were urban protests. Communities were upset about some specific problem but were little interested in structural change. They were outraged about government neglect or about their quality of life, but there was little in the way of awareness about the structural causes of their poverty. They wanted improvement but they seldom built up alliances with other neighbourhoods or with the labour movement.

How serious were these protests and what led to their becoming political issues? Access to land was certainly a factor in some social protests. In Santiago, the build-up to the 1970 election was dominated by a wave of land invasions. In 1970, no fewer than 103 invasions occurred in Santiago, many led by political parties from the Left, the eventual victors of the campaign. In Monterrey, left-wing parties also mobilised the population and encouraged them to occupy land. According to María Pozas-Garza (1989), 31 invasion settlements had been established by 1976. Together with 16 tenant organisations, three *ejido* communities, and three employment associations representing drivers, photographers and merchants these, settlements established an opposition front called *Land and Liberty*. For several years, this body ran the invasion settlements, pirating services, constructing schools and health clinics, and generally mobilising the population.

The demand for public services and for infrastructure was also a common stimulant to urban protest. During the 1970s a wave of civic strikes broke out in a series of small towns in Colombia; Santana (1983:135) believes 60 per cent of these were motivated principally by lack of water, electricity and drainage and a further 13 per cent by lack of decent transportation. In Monterrey, a widespread campaign was launched during the late 1970s and early 1980s to demonstrate for an adequate water system after drought had led to two consecutive summers of rationing. Vivian Bennett has documented how by July 1979, families from all social classes were involved, the middle class petitioning by phone, the poor in the streets, blocking roads and protesting outside government offices. In 1980, the central city was paralysed for two days running by irate housewives. There were protests outside the Governor's palace and in the low-income areas water trucks were seized along with their drivers. By the end of the year President López Portillo had declared the resolution of Monterrey's water problems to be a national priority.

Another likely source of settlement protest was the threat of forcible removal. A plan in the 1970s to build a motorway on the slopes of the mountains along the eastern edge of Bogotá threatened the demolition of a number of homes in an old established settlement. Backed by the main opposition party, the community protested and managed to force the government to modify the scheme. Similarly, in Mexico, there was vigorous opposition to urban renewal schemes during the late 1970s. A plan to widen major roads running through densely populated housing areas in the centre of the city was bitterly contested:

Largely middle-class in origin, local resident groups and defence committees arose in an attempt to prevent the land clearance necessary to create the grid of the proposed sixteen multi-lane highways. The groups that were formed enjoyed only minor success. One of the sixteen roads was shelved when injunctions served against the Federal District were upheld. Mostly, however, these failed or were sought too late when the bulldozers were tearing down houses (Ward, 1990:132).

Finally, natural disasters could sometimes mobilise the population to protest against the action or inaction of the authorities. Perhaps the most spectacular demonstrations following the earthquakes of 1985 in Mexico City.

After the Mexico City earthquake

The first earthquake hit Mexico City at 7.19 in the morning of 19 September 1985, a second following the next day. Most of the city was affected only slightly but terrible damage was sustained in the central area (Figure 7.1). While most of the historic buildings remained upright, a large number of

Figure 7.1
The earthquake in Mexico City: the main area affected

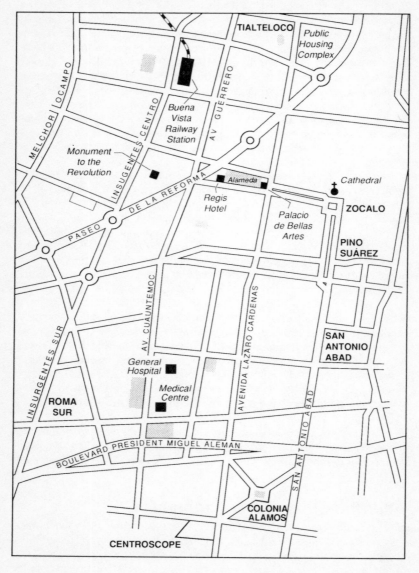

famous local landmarks did not. Among the buildings which were badly damaged were the National Medical Centre, the public housing complex at Tlatelolco, the Naval Ministry, the Ministry of Transport and Communications, the Juárez Hospital, and the Regis and Romano Hotels. Up to 90,000 homes may have been damaged, some 30,000 of which had to be demolished. No-one knows quite how many people died, but 10,000 remains a common estimate.

The residential areas most affected housed large numbers of tenants. Many had long been protected by rent controls and had lived for generations in the centre of the city. Tens of thousands were immediately made homeless, many more continued to live in buildings that were badly damaged. The authorities responded quickly, establishing a National Reconstruction Fund the next day and announcing an emergency housing programme on 30 September. By 11 October an extraordinary decree announced the expropriation of 5,448 properties damaged by the earthquake.

Such actions were not sufficient to stem a veritable wave of protests from those who had lost their homes. On 27 September, 3,000 people marched to the official home of the president (Los Pinos). Five days later 15,000 people demonstrated and three days after that large numbers of people from the Condesa, Doctores and Roma neighbourhoods held a meeting in the city's main square, the *Zócalo*. On 26 October, 30,000 victims marched to Los Pinos and three days later a further 6,000 people protested in the *Zócalo*. The demonstrations continued throughout November and on the 7 December 15,000 people again marched on Los Pinos. In March, people were still demanding action with 50,000 earthquake victims threatening to camp out in the main football stadium two months before the World Cup was scheduled to begin. The protesters were insisting that the government rehouse them in the same areas as they had been living.

The government's decision to expropriate property was a very radical step, but not one wholly unpopular with the owners, many of whom had been trying to rid themselves of the property and their tenants for many years. Much more surprising was the government's decision to rebuild homes in the central area and sell them at subsidised prices to the former tenants. In a highly efficient programme, nearly 50,000 new units were constructed. Most of the protesters were delighted at receiving such well-designed new homes in the central area, especially as they got them at highly subsidised prices.

Perhaps the Mexican experience shows that well-organised, large-scale protests can pressure Latin American governments into taking radical action. Even if the Mexican authorities had built new homes for the poor, they would not have subsidised them. But whether this would have happened in ordinary circumstances is another question. Mexican circum-

SUPERBARRIO

Superbarrio first made his appearance before the *Asamblea de Barrios* - an assembly of district groups, founded after the earthquake of 1985, committed to fighting evictions and to asserting people's rights to housing in Mexico City's shanty towns.

In July 1987 posters appeared throughout the city proclaiming the arrival of The Great Superbarrio, the defender of tenants and poor districts against the terror of grasping landlords. This symbolic fight was scheduled to take place in the open air in the city centre, until police confiscated the wrestling ring. Undaunted, Superbarrio again proclaimed the fight for 9 August in Tlatelolco, one of the areas worst hit by the earthquake, and successfully defeated his 'opponent'.

Superbarrio continues to lead protest marches and housing demonstrations, to impede evictions, and to attend open air meetings held each week by the *Asamblea de Barrios*. Agreements successfully negotiated with FONHAPO, a Government housing agency, have facilitated the building of hundreds of new homes.

"Of course, comparisons have been made with Superman," says Superbarrio. "But he derives his power from supernatural, non-intellectual sources. My power comes from Mexican popular culture and the popular imagination. Superbarrio doesn't face vampires or wolf-men; he faces flesh-and-blood landlords, politicians and bureaucrats, and he has no kryptonite to protect him."

Superbarrio represents the aspirations of thousands of ordinary people. In the ring he is a wrestler, on the streets he is a social fighter, yet all the while he remains a tenant.

Unpopular in right-wing circles, Superbarrio has also attracted criticism from the hard left on the grounds that he is not serious enough. Yet humour is Superbarrio's strongest weapon. People in power hate to look ridiculous. They sit behind mahogany desks, surrounded by deep-pile carpets. And then they get a visit from Superbarrio!

Adapted from Sayer (1991: 23-4).

stances were highly exceptional because the attention of the world's media was focused on Mexico City. Not only was there great sympathy with the people, but there was also anxiety about whether Mexico would be able to host the forthcoming World Cup football tournament. Financial support from the World Bank and developed countries helped reduced the cost of the programme. What the experience certainly shows is that the state is able

Superbarrio: Champion of Mexico City's poor   Julio Etchart/Reportage

to cope with major protests of this kind, that it can pacify demonstrators even during a recession. For, ultimately, the homeless accepted what they were offered and stopped protesting. They gladly accepted their subsidised homes and demanded nothing in the way of structural reforms.

The rise of new social movements

Despite the discovery of a great deal of urban protest, evidence of a concerted popular movement able or prepared to overturn reactionary regimes was thin on the ground. Castells, at least, accepted the evidence and backed away from his more radical statements about social movements. In *The city and the grassroots*, published in 1983, he concluded that in developing countries: "contrary to the expectations of those who believe in the myth of marginality and in spite of the fears of the world's establishment, social organization seems to be stronger than social deviance in these communities, and political conformism seems to outweigh the tendencies towards popular upheavals" (Castells, 1983: 175).

Yet no sooner had Castells recanted than scholars were pointing to new evidence which showed that the Latin American urban poor were busy mobilising, organising 'new social movements'. New hopes for change were excited by the community-based movements supported by the Church in Brazil, the collectives established in Chilean *campamentos*, and the widespread evidence of urban protests in Mexico. The sense of excitement is voiced by Sheldon Annis (1987:21) when he claims that:

> the poor today are better organized than ever before. Church groups, labor organizations, political action committees, village potable water associations, communal labor arrangements, cooperatives. Youth groups, squatter associations, worker-owned businesses. Ethnic burial societies, transportation collectives, peasant leagues. Catholic 'reflection' groups, tribal federations, microentrepreneur group credit associations...and on and on. In every Latin American country, such organizations pepper the social landscape, connecting the poor to each other and to their governments in unprecedented ways.

Surprisingly, it was the Church that had done most to help radicalise and motivate the poor to protest about their living conditions. The traditionally conservative Catholic Church became a rallying point, indeed the only safe rallying point, against the worst excesses of authoritarian government in Brazil, Chile and El Salvador. In the 1960s and 1970s, it was the Church that led protests against human rights abuses; it was the Church that most visibly led initiatives in social organisation and education. To the amazement of many, the Church had changed from being the most reliable bastion of support for the status quo to its most vociferous critic. Ever since a major meeting of the Latin American bishops in Medellín in 1968, the Church in many parts of Latin America had begun to adopt Liberation Theology. In Puebla in 1979, the Bishops had agreed to support a 'preferential option for the poor'. They would back Base Christian Communities (CEBs) which would use the Bible to make the poor conscious of injustice and to help them organise to change their lives. According to Alejandro Portes and Michael Johns (1986:286), "the Church's *comunidades de base* are thus found at the core of most recent successful mobilizations for political struggle or self-sufficiency in Argentina, Brazil, Chile and other South American countries".

The CEBs were especially important in Brazil, where some 100,000 groups were formed. They revitalised neighbourhood spirit and helped give communities a feeling of autonomy from the state. In Brazil, indeed, grassroots activism was an important factor in the undermining of the military regime. By combining neighbourhood demands for services with more generalised complaints about human rights, democracy, and corruption, the grassroots movement put moral pressure on the military. When neighbourhood associations started organising alliances, attended public demonstrations and announced their solidarity with trade unions on strike, political pressure mounted. Not only did such action affect the attitudes of the authorities but it also helped to change attitudes among the poor. As Paul Singer (1982:300) notes, with reference to São Paulo:

> What distinguishes the new neighbourhood movement from the old is that it springs from an inwardly focused effort: to develop a new consciousness, an attitude of unity for self-help among the population. The principal activities of the CEBs - mothers' clubs, mediation groups, study groups, communal shopping groups - all have this as an objective. The actions which are focused outwards stem from this attitude and the demands made assume the character of demands for rights and not for favours to be obtained by bargaining with the representatives of the state.

Unfortunately, there are signs that the Brazilian base community movement has become weaker since the demise of the military regime in 1985. Tilman Evers (1985) offers one possible explanation in interpreting the new social movements in Brazil as primarily a protest against power, a generalised reaction against any kind of central domination. With the demise of the military, the most obvious source of oppression disappeared. As a result, local groups lost interest in wider political questions, with the urban poor more interested in local issues. This tendency was accentuated by renewed party competition for votes from the communities, in which age-

WOMEN ORGANISE FOR CHANGE

Throughout urban Latin America there is evidence that women play a significant, often a leading role, in community organisation and protest. Burns' (1989) discussion of community action in a low-income settlement in the southeast of Mexico City reveals how this is both a method of pressurising the authorities for more resources and a way of changing accepted gender roles in the community.

"By day, San Miguel is a world of women and children. Men leave by the busload at dawn in search of a day's wage, and women are left to produce the miracle of survival, a task which has required collective action. For example, it was women, exasperated from washing babies, dishes, and laundry on a barrel of water a week, who stood for hours outside city hall demanding access to city water.

Women's involvement in the association set off hundreds of household 'revolutions', some negotiated, some violent, as women began to challenge their husbands' and in-laws' dictates and stepped out into new roles."

The organisation, *Mujeres en Lucha* (Women in Struggle), which had been founded by a handful of activists in 1982, became more and more effective as the economic recession deepened. It addressed critical issues such as the right to subsidised food and state help for their children. "For the first time, women not only filled the ranks of marches and sit-ins, but also negotiated demands with the authorities, and developed distribution systems for the resources they won (children's breakfast rations, milk cards, tortilla coupons, toys). By integrating consciousness-raising workshops into their organising process, they worked to ensure that women who first dared to step out of their house in search of cheaper tortillas stayed on to become an active part of the movement.

To challenge the consignment of women to unpaid labour in the home, women are organising community kitchens, laundries, and child-care centres where this work can be made more efficient, visible, collective, socially recognised, and eventually shared between men and women.

To dispel accusations that women's organising is divisive and to ensure that women's organising and issues do not become segregated within the movement as a whole, women have maintained what they call 'double militancy'. That is, they participate in twice as many meetings - developing a women's perspective in local and national women's meetings and then taking it to all the meetings of the organisation as a whole. Their objective is to place women's struggles at the very centre of the popular organisations that they are helping to build."

old techniques of populism and clientelism were reactivated. Today, as Scott Mainwaring (1989:195) puts it:

> Despite the intentions of movements to challenge them, populism and clientelism are alive and well in Brazilian society. The emergence of more autonomous, stronger popular movements in the second half of the 1970s did contribute to forcing political elites to change their discourse. The technocratic, authoritarian discourse of the most repressive period gave rise to a more participatory discourse. This change in itself is significant, but it should not camouflage the existence of populist practices. Nowhere was this so clear as in the state of Rio de Janeiro, with Governor Leonel Brizola.[2]

As a result, Mainwaring concludes that "many analyses of grassroots movements have erred on the side of exaggerating the novelty, strength, and autonomy of grassroots popular movements." Such analyses were also sometimes unclear about what precisely the 'new social movements' were. Attempts to categorise them were never very successful, and according to Schuurman and van Naerssen (1989:7) there is little evidence to suggest that they have either the ability or the desire to change the power structure. Perhaps Evers (1985) is right in arguing that they were mostly a sign of disenchantment, a spontaneous, unpredictable force rather than a consistent and unified movement capable of demanding real political change. An alternative interpretation is Annis' (1987:25) assessment that the new movements "hold more promise than ever before" and that they may now be "reaching some critical mass that will alter the fundamental relationships between the poor and their governments."

Protest during the recession

If most theorising about social movements has become more pessimistic about the opportunities for radical change, according to others the economic recession of the 1980s maintained grassroots activism. John Walton (1989:309), for example, has suggested that Latin America led "an unprecedented wave of international protest; unprecedented in the scope and essentially singular cause of a global protest analogous to earlier national strike waves. In frequency and vigor, the Latin American protests are distinct and provide the richest material for focused analysis of a global phenomenon."

If he is right, it would not be altogether surprising because Latin America has both a history of political organisation and bitter experience of austerity. What is distinctive about the recent austerity programmes in Latin America is not only their severity but also the speed with which they were

Table 7.1
Latin American austerity protests, 1976-87

CITY	DATE	ACTION	SEVERITY	PRECIPITATING EVENTS
ARGENTINA, BUENOS AIRES AND MENDOZA	March 1982 to August 1985	Demonstration by labour unions, strikes and looting	Hundreds arrested	Price increases, inflation and austerity policies
BOLIVIA, LA PAZ AND COCHABAMBA	March 1983 to March 1987	General strikes. Street violence, looting and protest marches	Proposed austerity package to increase prices of gasoline and food. Unemployment and devaluation	c10 killed, 1,500 arrested. Closure of mines, banks, shops, industry and universities
BRAZIL, SAO PAULO, RIO, BRASILIA AND OTHER MAJOR CITIES	April and October 1983	Riots over food prices, looting of supermarkets. Political protests	2 killed, 130 injured, 566 arrested	Devaluation, removal of subsidies, price increases
	November 1986 to July 1987	Violence, looting and vandalism. Peaceful general strike	Tens of injuries, 30 arrested	Renewed austerity, tax and price increases
CHILE, SANTIAGO AND VALPARAISO	March 1983 to September 1985	Regular political protests, general strikes	30-60 killed, over 1,000 arrests and several thousand detained	Devaluation, removal of subsidies, privatisation
ECUADOR, QUITO AND GUAYAQUIL	October 1982 to March 1987	General strikes, street violence and protests	Schools and universities closed. 7 killed, 50 wounded and 500 arrested	Price increase and removal of subsidies on flour, gasoline
PERU, VARIOUS	July 1976 to May 1985	Street riots and protests in Lima spreading to other cities. General strikes	21 killed and 'dozens' injured. 200 union officials arrested, 300-800 others arrested	Gasoline and food price increases, removal of subsidies, unemployment
EL SALVADOR, SAN SALVADOR	May 1985 to February 1986	Large protests by workers, students and teachers, public employees	Strikes, hospital taken over and 15 arrests	Price rises and university cuts. Later devaluation and austerity package
GUATEMALA, GUATEMALA CITY	September 1985	Riots, looting, protests and strikes	2-10 killed, 1,000 arrested. Troops invade university	Increase in bus fares, bread and milk prices
MEXICO, MEXICO CITY	February and May 1986	20-50,000 people in frequent protests	Some injuries	September 1985 earthquake and austerity
PANAMA, PANAMA CITY AND COLON	October 1983 and September 1985	General strike, protests, national assembly occupied	Tens of injuries, 30 arrested	Freeze on public sector wages and cuts in business subsidies

Source: Walton (1989)

introduced. It is this latter aspect that is particularly dangerous. As Paul Drake (1989:53-4) puts it: "It is that initial, sudden drop in resources, production and incomes that is most disruptive to governments. The subsequent slow, grueling process of adjustment and recuperation is much less destabilizing. After the original shock and plunge, expectations have been lowered. Persistent poverty seldom spawns upheaval."

But, how many 'austerity riots' have there been? Certainly, the outbreak of violence in Caracas in 1989 can be included in this category, but some instances in Walton's list (Table 7.1) seem to be somewhat debate-able. Some protests occurred before austerity programmes actually began, others, as in Chile, after years of austerity. Some protests were even triggered by some completely different event, such as the earthquakes in Mexico City. Some protests in the list took the form of strikes by organised labour movements against falling real wages or unemployment. Others were spontaneous outbreaks of violence against supermarkets or shops, as in São Paulo in 1983. Others were protests against a rise in fares, something which has led to buses or trains being burned for decades. If these are 'austerity riots' why have protests occurred in places where austerity has not been a major problem? In Colombia, for example, five relatively unsuccessful attempts were made to organise national strikes between 1977 and 1990, despite comparatively favourable economic conditions. Equally signifi-cantly, some countries where savage austerity programmes have been introduced have suffered from little unrest.

Mexico is a particularly interesting case in terms of the popular reaction to austerity. Between 1980 and 1988, Mexico City lost something like one-quarter of its manufacturing jobs. During that time, the minimum wage fell by around one-half, unemployment rose, and government subsi-dies were removed. Despite this draconian programme, the union move-ment rarely launched strikes and there was little sign of protest from the low-income settlements. As Susan Eckstein (1990a:176) declares, "austerity measures which have resulted in abrupt price increases in basic foods and transportation have not... given rise to riots, looting, street demonstrations, and other forms of protest."

The union movement's reaction to austerity has been somewhat perplexing throughout Latin America. General strikes were organised during the 1980s in Argentina, Bolivia, Chile, Colombia, Ecuador, Panama and Peru, but such events were not unknown in earlier times and it is by no means certain that they became more common. There has been a lot of union activism in Argentina, Brazil and Peru but factionalism has helped divide the union movement. Only in Bolivia where a brutal austerity programme led to the number of jobs in the state tin mining industry falling from 28,000 to 5,000 were the traditionally well-organised miners motivated to protest on a massive scale. In August 1986, they organised a march on La Paz from

'YESTERDAY CARACAS WAS BEIRUT'

"From six in the morning, dozens of passengers decided to occupy Avenida Lecuna [in the centre of Caracas] to protest against the fare rise. (See Figure 7.2.) The protest began quietly and several students from the Luis Caballero Mejías Polytechnic explained what had caused it: the government had approved a fare of 10 bolívares for the journey from Caracas to Guarenas and vice versa. To and from Guatire the fare would be 12 bolívares. But the drivers had decided unilaterally to charge 16 and 18 bolívares respectively without waiting for the Official Gazette to be published. They said that petrol prices had gone up on Sunday and they could not wait any longer.

From Avenida Lecuna the demonstrators moved towards Avenida Bolívar where, with their numbers growing, they felt stronger. There, at the exit of the tunnel, they built barricades and stopped the traffic. At first there were around two hundred people. Then a lot more gathered, shouting slogans against the general fare and price rises.

The Metropolitan Police looked on impassively as a number of buses were stopped. One of the officers explained that he had instructions not to shoot or take any action unless it was strictly necessary. Some officers were sympathetic and even supportive of the action, "we're also affected by the measures".

The traffic began to build up and the tailback stretched as far as the Parque Central and other junctions along the Avenida Bolívar. The traffic jam was becoming critical.

As the afternoon passed, more and more people were leaving their homes to take part in the protest. All the shops had closed and tension rose when dangerous objects began to be thrown out of the buildings of the Parque Central and the protesters threatened to retaliate.

It was dark when the morgue announced that several hospitals contained victims who had been shot dead. During the evening, columns of smoke were rising above the city, and people were walking home (public transport had been suspended and even the Metro had shut down); shots could be heard and looting of shops and vehicles broke out everywhere.

Yesterday Caracas was Beirut. Nobody had thought that the situation could go so far. Few had ever seen anything similar in the city, considered less than a month ago as the "centre" of world democracy. Tourists were watching amazed and taking photos. This is not what the travel agencies had portrayed. Nothing like this had occurred in thirty years of peace; people taking by force what they had been denied for decades. Everything exploded like a closed pressure cooker, its safety valve blocked by years of promises, corruption and immoral populism.

We spent all of the morning and part of the afternoon swallowing smoke and tear gas, dodging barricades, listening to insults and catching objects that came flying out of shop windows: packets of crisps, toilet paper, tooth paste and bottles of rum. Solidarity with the people forced us to take these as a sign of our 'commitment to the cause'.

The tour offered all kinds of surprises such as the soldier who was jealously guarding a large box of items given to him by grateful looters. And his colleague who was trying to conceal behind his back a teddy bear wrapped in cellophane.

Ordinary people know why the protests took place. The violence, with its appalling number of victims, has much to do with decades of corruption, growing poverty and unfilled promises. It has much to do with 'white collar' looting and the impunity with which it has been met.

Source: Fabricio Ojeda, *El Nacional* 28 and 29 February and 6 March 1989, reproduced in *SIC* and translated by the author.

Figure 7.2
Central Caracas

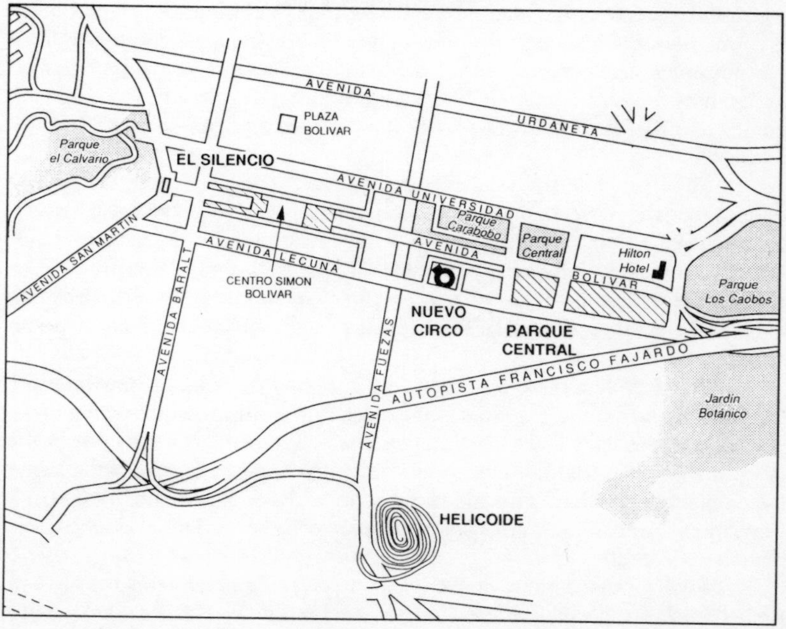

the mining city of Oruro, a distance of 150 miles. In alarm, the President ordered troops to surround the miners 28 miles from the Bolivian capital. After long negotiations, the miners decided to return to their camps. Later hunger strikes also failed to deflect the government from its chosen path and, despite fierce opposition, austerity won.

Three factors help to explain the failure of unions in most of Latin America to mount effective protests against austerity packages. The first is the general welcome given to the revival of democracy. Most union members realised that the new democratic governments had had no part in creating the economic mess that they were having to clear up. Unions also recognised that the new governments were being told what kinds of action they should take by outside organisations such as the International Monetary Fund and that few governments had much choice but to accept that advice.

The second reason for the muted response is that many unions had close links with the political parties which were often now in power. In Argentina, the unions form an important part of the Peronist movement and, in Venezuela, there is a strong alliance between the largest unions and the Democratic Action party. The failure of the Mexican unions to protest openly against the austerity programme, at least before 1992, was clearly linked to the intimate relationship between the ruling PRI and the Mexican Workers's Federation (CTM). The seemingly indestructible head of the CTM, Fidel Velásquez has long been a loyal supporter of Mexico's dominant party. While independent unions have become much stronger in recent years, Mexico's major cities have experienced remarkably few strikes. Throughout Latin America, the close ties between the unions and the main political parties have served to dampen protest at key moments.

Finally, while the loss of jobs has generated discontent it has also undermined the power of the trades unions and the resolve of those still in work to take strike action. A quantitative study of trade union activity in seven Latin American countries between 1976 and 1984 concluded that "rising joblessness clearly does have a measurable effect in discouraging strikes" (Epstein, 1989:177). Workers fearful of losing their jobs are much less likely to go on strike.

What protest there has been in Latin American cities has therefore usually come from the grassroots rather than trade unions or political parties. As Alejandro Portes (1990:36) argues, the recession "..has resulted in the gradual weakening of traditional organized movements, like trade unions, and the emergence of what Latin American scholars have dubbed the 'new social movements' - those made up of young people, women, residential associations, church-sponsored 'grass-roots' communities, and similar groups."

Such groups certainly have reason to protest and now that they live in more democratic societies are less intimidated by threats of force. Demonstrators are much less likely to face physical repression than under the more authoritarian regimes of the 1970s. At another level, protest may be contagious. Most Latin Americans now have television and can see what is going on in neighbouring countries. If the news tells them that their Venezuelan neighbours have protested against IMF programmes, there is some incentive to do the same.

But does this kind of protest mean that popular movements are seeking to overthrow the elitist alliances that still govern most countries? There is evidence that radical community organisations are establishing alliances across cities and even between cities, for example the National Coordinator of Popular Urban Movements (CONAMUP) movement in Mexico. However, there is also evidence that grassroots activity is being coopted in the traditional way. In Mexico, the government is successfully using populist rhetoric, negotiating with opposition movements, and offering selected groups rewards through its Solidarity Programme.

In many Latin American countries, therefore, governments have been extremely adept at defusing protest. Targetting programmes towards the most needy has formed an essential element in this strategy. In Chile, despite appalling increases in unemployment, cuts in general subsidies and decreasing expenditure on social programmes, targetting reduced the impact on the very poor. During the Pinochet dictatorship, "food distribution to pregnant mothers and to children under six, and special breakfast programs for children in the public primary schools...were implemented efficiently" (Meller, 1991:1559). These programmes did not win too many friends and General Pinochet's candidate lost the presidential election of 1990, but they did help dampen social protest.

In Bolivia, the government set up an Emergency Social Fund to help compensate for the effects of the austerity programme it was introducing. It funded projects presented to it by local government, NGOs and grassroots associations. The Fund "reached unprecedented numbers of poor, and fostered a cooperative relationship among local governments, organizations and the state for the first time. Groups traditionally in opposition discovered that they could benefit from working with the government. If this did not create direct suppport, it at least reduced potential opposition to the government and its program" (Graham, 1992:1244).

While austerity has had a terrible impact on urban living standards in most cities of Latin America, it cannot be denied that some governments have been highly effective in containing resulting conflict. Consequently, popular protest has broken out in few of the places where most predicted that it would.

What has happened, however, is that voters have sometimes turned against the traditional parties and elected new political formations to power. In Brazil, a woman candidate representing the Workers' Party was elected

HOW TO FEND OFF PROTEST: THE SOLIDARITY PROGRAMME IN MEXICO

Nowhere has the politics of containment been more skillfully employed than by the current Mexican administration. When Carlos Salinas de Gortari was elected in 1988 he was arguably the least popular president in Mexican history. He had won the election in very dubious circumstances and his party was widely accused of having engaged in electoral fraud. He lost decisively in Mexico City, voters in the national capital showing decisively how they felt about the way debt and austerity were undermining their living standards. Without changing Miguel de la Madrid's deflationary policies, policies of which as Minister of Budget and Planning he had been the main author, Salinas introduced a series of subtle social programmes to help the poorer groups in Mexican society.

His main weapon has been the Solidarity Programme (PRONASOL) which has become gradually more important during his period in office. PRONASOL's budget of US$820 million in 1989 rose to US$2.2 billion in 1992. The programme has several interesting features. First, it is run directly by the President and bypasses the existing bureaucracy. This improves the prospects of the funds being spent efficiently and most importantly keeps control in the hands of the President (he appointed his own brother to run the programme). Second, much of the assistance has so far been given to groups which were affiliated to parties opposed to the President's own party, the PRI. He has undermined left-wing opposition by signing agreements with popular organisations and offering them important benefits through the PRONASOL programme. As one of those left-wing groups admitted in 1989, PRONASOL's budget while clearly inadequate to deal with the needs of Mexico's 40 million poor and 17 million severely poor, was large enough "to employ the politics of cooptation, to manipulate demands and to give the appearance of attending to the needs of the poor."[3]

The programme's success is perhaps best demonstrated in the upgrading of the Chalco area in the southeast of Mexico City. This immense area of irregular housing lacked piped water, electricity and sewerage. Water was provided by privately operated water tankers which ran local monopolies. In 1989, PRONASOL installed electricity and water in a large part of the district. The project was inaugurated by the President in September and skillful play was made of his spending the night in the colonia. He was pictured talking to the inhabitants next morning, asking them if they were happy with the project. The television audience was left in little doubt that they were delighted.

Third, the programme uses targetted subsidies in place of the general subsidies traditionally employed by Mexican governments. General food subsidies, which had cost the equivalent of one per cent of national product in 1983, accounted for only 0.02 per cent of GDP by the end of 1986. In their place, targetted subsidies were introduced. PRONASOL now distributes coupons to poor families with children, entitling them to one free kilo of tortillas a day. In addition, an existing programme to provide subsidised milk to the poor was expanded. The milk is distributed between 5.30am and 8.00am from special sites in low-income areas.

Mayor of São Paulo. In Colombia, former guerrillas from the M-19 held majority power in the 1991 Constituent Assembly. In Mexico, the dominant PRI has conceded state governorships to the opposition PAN in Baja California, Chihuahua and Guanajuato. In Peru, a left-wing candidate, Alfonso Barrantes was elected Mayor of Lima in 1984 and the rank outsider and 'non-politician' Alberto Fujimori to the presidency in 1990. In Venezuela, the left-wing populist party Causa-R has recently won power in the cities of Caracas and Ciudad Guayana.

These victories certainly do not suggest that there will be a vast movement to the left in Latin America, as the success of the right-wing PAN party in Mexico and President Fujimori's popularly endorsed 'self-inflicted coup' illustrate. What they do suggest, however, is that recession, austerity and new forms of popular organisation are having a strong and often unpredictable impact on Latin American politics.

Notes

(1) In 1977, of the twenty Latin American governments, only those in Colombia, Costa Rica, Mexico and Venezuela had been elected. Even among these the Colombian government was still maintaining a coalition between the two main parties and the influence of the military was growing. In Mexico, where the PRI had provided the winning presidential candidate ever since 1929, the country was effectively a one-party state.

(2) Leonel Brizola was Governor of the State of Rio de Janeiro from 1982 to 1986. As leader of the Democratic Workers' Party, he adopted a strongly populist stance.

(3) Asamblea de Barrios, document prepared for the 1st National Urban Popular Convention, 1989. Cited in Haber (1992).

Further reading

For interesting discussions of the politics of land invasion in Chile, see Castells (1983), Cleaves (1974), Kusnetzoff (1975) and Rodríguez (1989).

For a discussion of the reaction to urban displacement in Bogotá, see Revéiz *et al.* (1977) and Janssen (1978).

The political reaction to the 1985 earthquake in Mexico City has been extensively documented. See Connolly (1990), Coulomb and Duhau (eds.) (1988), Eckstein (1990a and 1990b), Villa (1987) and Ward (1990).

Examples of urban protests and the role of the popular sector are discussed in the following: in Brazil, Boran (1989), Evers (1985), Kowarick (ed.) (1988) and Singer (1982); in Chile, Kusnetzoff (1990), Oxhorn (1991) and Schneider (1991); in Colombia, Cabrera *et al* .(1986), Santana (1989) and Pearce (1990); and in Mexico, Bennett (1989), Coulomb and Duhau (eds.) (1989) and Haber (1990). General theories about social movements and protests are discussed by Slater (ed.) (1985).

For discussions of trade union activity during the recession of the 1980s, see Beijaard (1992), Drake (1989), Epstein (1989), Palmer (1992) and Roxborough (1989).

8

THE FUTURE
OF THE CITY

Despite all cataclysmic forecasts made over its future, the Latin American city has survived. For all the reversals of the 1980s, the city still has a future, even an optimistic one. Latin American cities are not going to disintegrate due to social violence or physical disaster. They are not going to be overwhelmed by masses of ill-educated rural people, nor are they are going to be swept away by urban insurgencies or terrorism. Instead, most will increasingly look like the poorer cities of the United States and Western Europe.

Even if prospects of urban chaos can be discounted, it is less than certain that every city faces a pleasant future. There are some real problems ahead, most importantly the question of whether there will be enough jobs to satisfy the burgeoning labour force. If this is a general problem throughout the region, other difficulties are more locally specific. Because there is no typical Latin American city, there can be no single urban future. Some cities will prosper over the next twenty years, whereas the prospects for others are distinctly dim.

National economic growth

Any country which is suffering from an economic recession will have difficulty in providing enough jobs and decent housing for its inhabitants. It will also have problems in providing sufficient infrastructure and services. Economic growth is a necessary, if hardly a sufficient, basis for raising the quality of urban life.

The 1980s was a disastrous decade for most Latin American countries and certainly for most of their cities. Not only did per capita income decline in virtually every country, but the urban areas bore the brunt of the recession. After years of getting much more than their fair share of the growing cake, even the crumbs were disappearing fast during the 1980s. The impact of the recession on Latin America's cities was profound, and even

Figure 8.1
Latin America: economic growth, 1977-1992

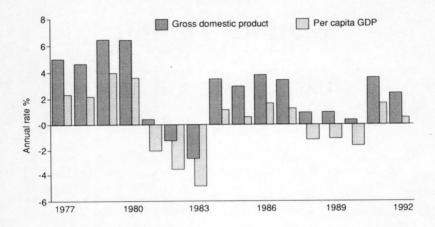

Source: UNECLAC (1992)

now some of the negative consequences are still partially hidden.

Fortunately, the economic prospects for Latin America in the 1990s are rather better. Figure 8.1 shows that 1991 and 1992 represented a distinct improvement on most of the 1980s, and certainly on the periods 1981-1983 and 1988-1990. Better prospects, however, are not consistent across the region. As Table 8.1 shows, the recent growth record of the region's largest countries is highly variable. Judging from recent experience, there are reasons to be optimistic in Argentina, Chile, Mexico and Venezuela, but considerable grounds for pessimism in Brazil and Peru. Should current trends continue, most cities in the expanding economies should experience a lessening of their economic problems; in Brazil and Peru there is likely to be a continued loss of jobs and investment. The local urban future is heavily dependent on national economic trends.

The changing international division of labour

Over the last twenty years, Latin America has increased its level of participation in the world economy. Most Latin American governments have encouraged this trend and have been strongly supported from Washington. In order to improve Latin America's economic performance, a similar package of measures has been adopted in most parts of the region.

Table 8.1
Economic growth in selected Latin American countries, 1980-1992
(Annual growth in GDP)

COUNTRY	1980 to 1984	1985 to 1989	1990 to 1992
ARGENTINA	-3	-2.3	1.1
BRAZIL	-0.5	2.5	-2.6
CHILE	-0.1	4.8	4.2
COLOMBIA	-1.5	3	1.3
MEXICO	-0.6	-1.2	1.4
PERU	-2.4	-2.5	-3.8
VENEZUELA	-3.5	-0.9	6.1

Source: UNCECLAC

The conventional wisdom has been that Latin America should seek to export more to the world market. To do this, governments should devalue the national currency, make their exports more competitive and encourage local companies to seek out foreign markets. Many governments have done this successfully, as Table 8.2 demonstrates. With the exception of Brazil and Peru, exports have increased dramatically when measured against the growth of gross national products. Table 8.2 also shows that, between 1965 and 1990, the composition of these exports changed: every country managed to increase its exports of manufactured products. Latin America's exports no longer consist only of minerals and agricultural produce.

A second element in the integration of Latin America into the world economy has been the opening up of its markets to imports. Country after country has cut its previous level of protection. In Mexico, the average tariff on imports fell from 45 per cent in 1987 to 9 per cent in 1992. In Colombia, the average level of effective protection fell from 75 per cent in December 1989 to 26 per cent two years later; locally produced consumer goods now receive only 15 per cent protection. The cut in levels of protection is intended to make local industry and agriculture more efficient. Protected for years by high tariff walls and a distorted exchange rate, all kinds of inefficient industrial practices developed. Liberalisation, according to current economic orthodoxy, will rid the region of many of these undesirable traits.

In the future, the local consequences of stronger integration into the world economy will certainly vary between countries. Some will be able to

Table 8.2
Export production in Latin America (per cent), 1965-1990

COUNTRY	EXPORTS/GNP		MANUFACTURES/	EXPORTS
	1965	1990	1965	1990
ARGENTINA	8	14	6	35
BRAZIL	8	7	8	53
CHILE	14	37	4	10
COLOMBIA	11	20	7	26
MEXICO	8	16	16	44
PERU	26	11	1	16
VENEZUELA	26	39	2	11

Source: World Bank (1992a: 234-5 and 248-9)

compete on the world market while others will fail. Whereas Chile, Colombia and Mexico may well respond well to international competitive forces, it is very unlikely that Bolivia, Peru and several of the Central American republics will be as successful.

It cannot even be assumed that freer trade will bring major benefits for the more successful countries. For if most Latin American countries have shown that they can increase exports of raw materials and some have managed to export manufactured products, there are still several clouds on the horizon. First, the world economy is currently in recession. Demand for both raw materials and manufactures has been in decline. Should the recession continue, the prospects for Latin American exports will be severely damaged. Second, there are signs that the developed countries are becoming more protectionist. President Clinton is under strong pressure to cut back on manufactured imports and the European Community has been discouraging agricultural imports from Latin America for several years. How can Latin America increase its exports if levels of protection are increasing? Third, how will Latin American countries cope with increasing foreign competition in their domestic markets? Will their domestic farmers be able to compete with imported grain from the United States, and how will their industries cope with the onslaught of cheap Japanese manufactures? If domestic manufacturing and, in places, domestic agriculture cannot com-

Figure 8.2
Maquila employment on the US-Mexico border area, 1990

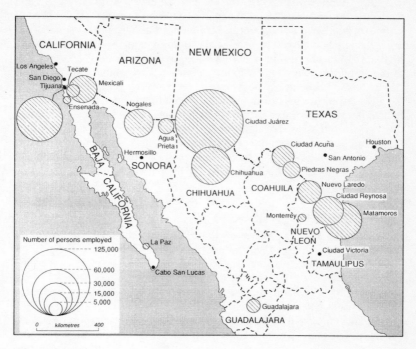

pete with imports, what are the future prospects for economic growth and employment generation?

Even where liberalisation leads to faster economic growth, we should not assume that every urban area will benefit, as the local impact of liberalisation is likely to differ considerably. Mexico already provides a good illustration of the variable impact of this process. From the late 1980s, Mexico shifted from being one of Latin America's most protected countries to one of its most open. It continues to follow this strategy because it has the advantage, at least if the strategy proves to be a correct one, of sharing a two-thousand mile border with the world's largest economy.

In the last decade, two major changes occurred in Mexico. First, devaluation of the currency allowed industry and agriculture in the border areas to increase sales to the United States. The number of *maquiladoras* in Mexico increased from 448 in 1976 to 1,936 in 1990 and employment increased from 75,000 in 1976 to 540,000 in 1993. During the 1980s, new export plants were also set up by major vehicle companies in towns such as Chihuahua, Hermosillo and Saltillo, all some distance from the frontier. Together, the new plants of Chrysler, Ford, General Motors, Nissan and Renault produced over 350,000 vehicles for export in 1992. If the pace of growth of *maquila* employment and production has been phenomenal, it has only partially helped to resolve Mexico's employment problems. As Harley Shaiken (1990:122) points out, total *maquila* employment is "less than half of the amount by which the Mexican labor force expands each year".

Second, liberating the Mexican economy by removing protection has also led to the loss of many jobs in manufacturing, as imports have helped put uncompetitive manufacturing plants out of business. Although the domestic recession has contributed, employment in the factories of the major cities of the interior has plummeted, and many small workshops have also gone out of business. The overall result of liberalisation in Mexico, therefore, has been to change profoundly the pattern of industrial location in the country.

Demographic pressure

Latin America's urban prospects will be helped by the fact that most cities will grow more slowly. This tendency was already apparent in the 1980s when the combined forces of falling rates of fertility and economic recession slowed the pace of urban expansion. World Bank figures (1990; 1992) show that during the 1980s, urban areas grew annually by 3.0 per cent compared to 3.9 per cent between 1965 and 1980.

This trend is likely to continue in the future for a number of reasons. Firstly, as Chapter Two showed, fertility rates have been declining rapidly in most countries. Lower fertility rates will both slow natural population growth in the city and reduce cityward migration by lowering demographic pressure in the countryside. These trends will be reinforced by the fact that increasing numbers of Latin Americans seem to be moving to developed countries. Durand and Massey (1992) estimate the number of undocumented Mexicans living in the United States in 1986 at around 3.1 million. Large numbers of Cubans, Dominicans, Central Americans, Colombians and Puerto Ricans have also moved to the United States. In total, some five million undocumented Latin Americans may have moved to the United States during the 1980s (United Nations, 1989). Increasingly, too, there are signs that more Latin Americans are moving to Europe.

Second, it is likely that the populations of some of the major cities of Latin America will increase more slowly in the future because their economic prospects are less favourable than those of many smaller cities. Again, there were clear signs of such a trend in Mexico during the 1980s. The shift in development strategy from import substitution to export

Air pollution in Mexico City   Julio Etchart/Reportage

orientation took away the major advantage that Mexico City had previously held over other cities in the country. The decline of industrial employment in Mexico City when compared with the dynamism of the border cities is ample testimony to this shift in comparative advantage.

Third, the larger cities of Latin America are likely to grow more slowly in the future for environmental and economic reasons. Latin American companies are gradually realising the difficulties that they face by operating in the mega-cities. They are forced to pay more for land, suffer from worse traffic congestion and often have to pay higher labour costs than if they were operating from some other location. In response, some manufacturing firms have been establishing branch plants outside the major cities, a trend particularly noticeable around Buenos Aires, Mexico City, Rio de Janeiro and São Paulo. In most cases they are not moving their factories very far, setting up within 100 miles of the major city and thereby maintaining access to the largest national market while gaining from cheaper costs of land and labour in the nearby city. With the improvement of roads and infrastructure in the regions surrounding the major cities, this trend towards a deconcentrated urban form is bound to accelerate.

Perhaps the only factor that is likely to counter these trends towards slower metropolitan expansion is what is happening in the countryside. In certain parts of Latin America, changing rural conditions could lead to accelerated cityward migration. In places, rural violence may encourage more people to move to the comparative safety of the cities. In Peru, the activities of the Shining Path guerrillas and the countermeasures of the military have made large areas of the southern highlands extremely danger-ous, and there is ample evidence that Lima has been receiving large numbers of refugees from the *sierra*. In Colombia, the activities of the military, the guerrillas and the drug dealers have also made it extremely difficult to live in large swathes of the countryside.

In addition, large cities may receive more migrants as a result of economic forces operating in the countryside. In some areas, commerciali-sation has been growing apace and agricultural production has increased dramatically. The efforts of fruit producers in Chile and in northwest Mexico have been very impressive in this regard. For some this has created work and raised incomes, but raising productivity is not a guarantee that all will get jobs. Indeed, there are signs that the opposite has been occurring in many areas. In Brazil, where the acreage devoted to sugar has increased in response to the policy of fuelling more cars with gasohol, large numbers of small-scale tenant farmers have been displaced from the land. Recently, Mexico has reformed its agrarian legislation so that commonly held prop-erties, *ejidos,* can in future be rented or sold. The authorities hope that this will lead to a major increase in rural investment but recognise that it may lead to many losing access to their land. If cheap maize from the United States is permitted to enter Mexico under the auspices of the North American Free Trade Agreement, the effect on 2.4 million small-scale maize producers will be profound. A major move to the cities will be an inescapable response to any undercutting of Mexican agriculture's staple product.

In general, urban expansion is likely to slow in the 1990s, and especially in the largest cities. On balance, migration should be a less significant factor in urban expansion than it has been in the past. At the same time, in certain parts of Latin America local economic and social processes may actually lead to faster migration to the cities.

Urban employment

During the 1980s, both unemployment and underemployment became more serious. The recession cut the number of formal sector jobs at a time when the numbers of young Latin Americans entering the labour force had never been higher. While recession should constitute less of a problem in most countries during the 1990s, the prospects in terms of urban employment are very worrying. First, the pressure to shed manufacturing jobs in order to raise productivity is continuing. The opening up of Latin America's markets to overseas competition will lead to the closure of many local factories and to production cut-backs in others. Jobs will be shed as companies invest in more modern forms of technology. William Cline (1991) has estimated that a further 10 million manufacturing jobs may be lost during the 1990s.

Second, the public sector is most unlikely to compensate for this trend by recruiting on a large scale. Indeed, with the dogma of privatisation, cost recovery and balanced budgets now adopted by most Latin American governments, the long-held belief that there are too many public employees has been transformed into the policy goal of cutting back government workers. During the 1990s, many more government jobs could be cut. Given that public sector jobs account for one-fifth of all jobs in Latin America, such cuts would mean the displacement of between 5 and 10 per cent of the workforce (Iglesias, 1992:116).

Any job losses, even if economic growth manages to create new jobs, are likely to prove a huge problem at a time when large numbers of young people are seeking to enter the work force. In 1990, approximately 40 million urban people were aged between 10 and 14. Before the year 2000 most of these will want some kind of job. It is very doubtful whether Latin America's cities can produce enough employment opportunities to satisfy them.

Governance

Improving the quality of 'governance' is currently high on the political agenda in both Latin America and Washington D.C. The political will now exists to remedy some of the inefficiency that bedevils the public sector. While the current approach runs the danger of cutting the public sector to the bone, reform is undoubtedly necessary if government is to play its proper role in Latin America. But what precisely is this role? The World Bank (1992b:1) argues that:

> good governance is central to creating and sustaining an environment which fosters strong and equitable development, and it is an essential complement to sound economic policies. Governments play a key role in the provision of public goods. They establish the rules that make markets work efficiently and, more problematically, they correct for market failure. In order to play this role, they need revenues, and agents to collect revenues and produce the public goods. This in turn requires systems of accountability, adequate and reliable information, and efficiency in resource management and the delivery of public services.

In one respect at least, the prospects for better governance in Latin America do not look bad. Good governance clearly requires both political stability and democratic participation. On both counts, most of Latin America has improved remarkably over recent years. Few countries in the region are suffering from political instability. Political violence is a problem only in Colombia, Guatemala and Peru, and only the presidents of Guatemala and Venezuela are in serious danger of being displaced by a military coup. For good or ill, there is little possibility of a social revolution in most parts of the region. There has also been a strong trend towards democratic government in recent years. The military regimes that dominated in most countries in the 1970s gave way to civilian regimes during the 1980s. While there are signs of a shift backwards in Peru and Venezuela, it is a long time since a form of democratic government was quite so well established in the region. Much to everyone's shock, "the truly surprising story into the late 1980s was the survivability of these rickety political systems under extremely inauspicious economic circumstances" (Drake, 1989:53).

Of course, political instability is incompatible with the concept of good governance. In Peru, the activities of the Shining Path guerrilla movement and the brutal reaction of the military have led to large numbers of people fleeing from the violence of the rural areas. It has also led to violence in Lima as the guerrillas have assassinated local leaders and carried out terrorist attacks. The recent capture of the movement's leader, Abimael Guzmán, has encouraged the authorities to believe that they are winning the battle. If they are wrong, then major difficulties will ensue, and with them, the prospects for economic growth and orderly urban development will diminish.

Similarly, Colombia has a major security problem. This stems in part from guerrilla activity, but much of the violence is also associated with drugs. The two problems are connected insofar as some guerrillas are financing their operations through drug dealing and some drug dealers are pretending that they have political aspirations, thereby justifying their use of violence. Either way, both groups are capable of inflicting considerable damage on the national economy, the rural areas and the cities. One guerrilla group has been regularly blowing up the country's oil pipelines, something which threatens its export earnings. Pablo Escobar, the head of the Medellín drug cartel, is thought to have been responsible for a series of recent bomb explosions in Bogotá. Meanwhile, his opponents have been attacking his family and property in and around Medellín. Insofar as either guerrillas or drug cartels are successful in disrupting urban life, there is a question mark over the future development of Colombia's cities.

If political instability and violence are not major problems in most countries of the region, their absence does not necessarily guarantee good governance. Major reforms are overdue and changes in seemingly age-old governmental practices are required. Fortunately, there are some signs that some Latin American governments are implementing positive changes, especially in the urban arena. Mexico City, for example, is beginning to control its air pollution and to curb some of its excessive numbers of cars. Despite the recession, the administration has managed to increase distribu-

Lima: shanty town populated by refugees from rural violence　　Julio Etchart/Reportage

tion of water and electricity. There was even the miracle of a two-week period in Mexico City when the police were persuaded not to extract bribes from car drivers! In Curitiba, Brazil, there are excellent signs that at least one urban administration is acting competently. Even though Vicente del Rio (1992) suggests that the merits of Curitiba's administration may have been turned into some kind of 'urban myth', the example it is giving in terms of transport planning and garbage collection is highly positive.

Unfortunately, such examples of good urban government are still the exceptions. Good governance is anything but obvious in most cities of Latin America. It is certainly not very apparent in some of the border cities of northern Mexico where sewage and industrial waste is pouring into the Rio Grande. It is less than evident in São Paulo where increasing levels of street crime and a generalised lack of confidence in the justice and police systems lead Lucio Kowarick (1991) to label Brazil's largest city the 'metropolis of industrial underdevelopment'. It is far from obvious in Peru as the state of public services deteriorates in the nation's capital (Riofrío, 1991). The dangers of poor government are clear from Simon Strong's description of Lima:

Cholera symbolized Peru's social, economic and even psychological malaise. The disease bred on the country's hunger and rottenness. And

CURITIBA: A LATIN AMERICAN URBAN PANACEA?

Curitiba is probably the most lauded city in Latin America. Its example is heralded as the lesson that most other urban areas must learn. *The Economist* (April 17, 1993) praised the "simple and cheap measures that have turned Curitiba into one of the country's most agreeable cities." Michael Cohen, head of the Urban Development Division at the World Bank has said that: "In our judgement Curitiba is one of the most exciting places in the world. There is a move towards a better integration of policy and practice than in virtually any place we have seen. It is worth understanding and following up" (Harris, 1992:59). In Brazil, Curitiba's physical solutions, particularly those related to transportation, have become 'planning standards' and have been copied in the most remote towns. What is so impressive about the way that the city has been run?

According to Vicente del Rio (1992:275-7): "Curitiba is perhaps the only major Brazilian city where growth and expansion processes have been tackled by comprehensive planning in the last two decades. The Urban Planning and Research Institute (IPPUC) was created at the end of the 1960s as a political means towards flexibility and dynamism, bypassing the bureaucracy of city departments. Born at the peak of the military regime when there was a strong belief in functional 'technocratic' planning, one of IPPUC's objectives was to 'change the looks of the city and to prepare it for the future'. Having survived the vagaries of national politics, it became the most important agency in Curitiba as a laboratory for new urban projects, praised for originality and effectiveness but whose success has yet to be critically appraised.

This success is largely due to architect Jaime Lerner, who has been mayor for three terms of office. With his small and innovative team based at IPPUC, Lerner succeeded in implementing simple and workable ideas that depended, to a large extent, on his popularity and political gamesmanship. Part of this popularity was created from projects and programmes during his first mandate, many of which had been recommended in the original master plan. Now they cover a wide spectrum including special zoning for industrial districts, public transportation systems, preservation and image building, community participation, environmental programmes for recycling garbage, and many others.

Planners have succeeded in providing faster and safer vehicle circulation by means of a three-lane system with separate lanes for buses and cars. The *ligeirinho* ('speedy') buses collect passengers from special reinforced-plastic tubular sheds, whose architectural design, though far from perfect, makes boarding and exiting faster and more comfortable with higher efficiency at much lower costs than more sophisticated public mass transit systems.

Curitiba was seen throughout Brazil as an *avant garde* city in the early 1970s, when it decided to create pedestrian precincts downtown with complementary landscaping. The *calçadao* (big sidewalk) of *Rua das Flôres* quickly turned into a lively meeting place with cafes, shops, cultural activities and colourful flower stalls. Shoppers could leave their children in the care of city recreation officials in a converted old tram that also offered special education programmes at weekends.

Next to *Rua das Flores*, another recent urban innovation is the *Rua 24 Horas* which occupies the heart of an inner-city block. A pedestrianised street with shops and cafes covered by a cast-iron and glass arcade, it stays open day and night.

Curitiba has recently received the title of 'environmental capital of Brazil' owing to its 50 sq.m. of green space per capita and for its programme of collecting and recycling urban waste. The programme receives special emphasis in the *favelas* where squatters get bags of food in exchange for their garbage.

Curitiba's experience teaches the importance and the feasibility of simple - not simplistic - urban design. Recently, Mayor Lerner stated that 'the city of the future will look a lot like the cities of today. We have to get the grandiose solutions out of our heads.' He is right in that the time of grand schemes seems definitely to be over. There is insufficient money for one thing, and full democracy should guarantee effective and widespread public expenditure. Curitiba is 'small is beautiful' revisited, where good political sense and the maximisation of the spiral effect of small actions are fundamental."

like the war it partnered, its victims were mostly those whom the state had long ago abandoned.

Around the packed streets in downtown Lima near the increasingly anomalous features of the presidential palace and congress, the nauseating smell of urine, rotting fruit and burning rubbish cloyed the air. Most of the lower windows of the ministry of finance had been smashed by rocks. As manhole covers were stolen for scrap - causing children to fall in and materialize several kilometres away in the River Rimac, drowned in sewage - gaping holes opened up in the roads where water and sewage pipes had burst underneath. Sewage seeped into the water. Traffic grew ever more congested not because there were more cars or even buses to relieve the chronic pressure on Lima's battered and choked public transport, but because the street sellers had expanded from the pavements into the inside lanes.

Clearly, better government is imperative if Latin America's urban population is to benefit from economic growth. Without it, infrastructure and service provision will not expand, which will in turn prevent self-help builders from improving their housing conditions. Without good government, transport systems will continue to deteriorate leading to worsening traffic congestion and longer journeys to work. Without better administered taxation systems, there will be too few funds to supply health and education services to the poor. The challenge is there; it remains to be seen whether the political will exists to meet it.

Repaying the social debt

The crisis of the 1980s led to a major increase in poverty in Latin America. "Based on conservative estimates, the percentage of poor people rose from 41 per cent in 1980 to 44 per cent in 1989 - that is, to 183 million inhabitants" (Iglesias, 1992:103). Much of that poverty was concentrated in Latin America's cities. Indeed, according to UNECLAC (1990), 104 million poor people lived in urban areas, some 36 per cent of the total urban population. Although the proportion of rural people living in poverty continued to be much higher, at 61 per cent, rising poverty was a new phenomenon for the cities. During the 1980s, most urban dwellers suffered from falling wages, rising levels of unemployment and underemployment, and declining investment. In addition, most governments cut back on social expenditure. Even when social spending's share of the budget was maintained, government expenditure in real terms fell dramatically. Since most of the social budget went into current expenditure, there was a major cut in investment in the fields of education, health and social welfare.

Should such a trend continue in the 1990s, there is a real danger that urban poverty will become endemic. If education and health programmes are not improved, the progress that was made during the 1960s and 1970s in terms of literacy, infant mortality and life expectancy will come under threat. The danger is clearly recognised by the Inter-American Development Bank, perhaps the most significant actor in Washington in the light of cutbacks in World Bank lending to Latin America. In planning its lending programme for the 1990s the Bank is arguing for a much greater emphasis on social investment than previously:

> This greater emphasis of Bank programs on social investment is justified by the high level of unmet demand, as well as the low investment levels registered in social areas in recent years. Deterioration of social sector infrastructure, institutions and delivery systems has resulted in a deceleration of the pace of improvement in social indicators which, if not corrected, may lead to reversals of these indicators (Inter-American Development Bank, 1992a:22).

If other lenders and Latin America's own governments do not increase social expenditure, then real urban problems could lie in wait.

Income inequality

Latin America has long been a highly unequal region. This is manifest both in the unequal land holding systems of the countryside and in the vast gulf in living conditions that exists between the affluent and poor areas of every Latin American city. During the 1980s, levels of inequality undoubtedly increased. The very rich protected themselves through buying dollars or investing in real estate. The urban middle class and the poor suffered as they lost their jobs or as inflation eroded their incomes. Unless policies are enacted to remedy the current levels of inequality, there is a real danger that resentment will overflow.

What form that resentment may take is unpredictable. In places, it will lead to increasing rates of crime; elsewhere it may lead to riots in the streets or to the looting of shops. In some cases, it will lead to massive electoral support for populist leaders, elsewhere to general apathy. Whatever the response, governments will have to take action to remove some of the main grounds for protest. In the past, governments have managed to suppress political resentment through a clever mix of carrots and sticks. Today's urban population is much more sophisticated, however, and may react less favourably to populist gestures than in the past. While it would be unwise to predict a future of urban upheaval, a failure to respond to the issue of economic and social inequality will bring such an outcome immeasurably closer.

* * * * * * *

In general, Latin America's cities face a much more optimistic future than do cities in most parts of Africa or those in many parts of Asia. But much depends on the rate of economic growth, without which it is difficult to improve most people's lives, and much on better and fairer government. Since these factors will vary from country to country, what will happen in one city is very unlikely to happen in precisely the same way anywhere else. Where opportunities to increase manufactured exports are grasped, well-remunerated jobs may increase; where imported manufactures displace local production, levels of unemployment may rise. What the future will bring depends both upon the local prospects for growth and upon the way governments channel their resources into equitable social programmes. Both economic growth and poverty alleviation policies are needed. Without either, the future for some cities in Latin America could yet turn out to be extremely bleak.

Further Reading

Good resumés of Latin America's economic problems and prospects are presented annually in the annual review produced by the Inter-American Development Bank *Economic and Social Progress in Latin America and the Caribbean.*

On Latin America's changing role in the international economy, see Gwynne (1990) and Harris (1987).

For discussion of the development of the *maquilas* along the US-Mexico border, see Bortz (1991), Philip (ed.) (1988: chs. 10-11), Sklair (1989), Shaiken (1990) and South (1990). On the urban problems faced along the US-Mexico border, see Herzog (1991). On the state of public services and public order in Lima, see Riofrío (1991) and Strong (1992). On the problems of São Paulo, see Kowarick (1991).

On the nature of urban governance, see Gilbert (1992), Harris (ed.) (1992), World Bank (1992b) and World Bank (1991).

On ways to help reduce urban poverty in Latin America, see Iglesias (1992) and World Bank (1992c).

BIBLIOGRAPHY

Abrams, C. (1964) *Man's struggle for shelter in an urbanizing world*, MIT Press.
Acevedo, J. (1990) 'El transporte en Bogotá', in Suárez, H. (ed.) *Vivir en Bogotá*, Ediciones Foro Nacional.
Alba, C. (1986) 'La industrialización en Jalisco: evolución y perspectivas', in de la Peña, G. and Escobar, A. (eds.) *Cambio regional, mercado de trabajo y vida obrera en Jalisco*, El Colegio de Jalisco, 89-146.
Annis, S. (1987) 'Reorganization at the grassroots: its origins and meaning', *Grassroots Development* 11, 21-25.
Arias, P. and Roberts, B.R. (1985) 'The city in permanent transition: the consequences of a national system of industrial specialization', in Walton, J. (ed.) *Capital and labour in the industrialized world*, Sage, 149-75.
Austin, A.G. and Lewis, S. (1970) *Urban government for metropolitan Lima*, Praeger.
Avello, D.J. *et al.* (1989) *Constructores de ciudad*, Ediciones Sur.
Azuela, A. (1989) *La ciudad, la propiedad privada y el derecho*, El Colegio de México.

Balán, J., Browning, H.L. and Jelín, E. (1973) *Men in a developing society: geographic and social mobility in Monterrey, Mexico*, University of Texas Press.
Balderas, J. and Molero, E. (1988) 'Sistema eléctrico en la ciudad de México', in Garza, G. (ed.) *Atlas de la ciudad de México*, DDF and El Colegio de México, 179-83.
Batley, R. (1982) 'Urban renewal and expulsion in São Paulo', in Gilbert, A.G., Hardoy, J.E. and Ramírez, R. (eds.), 191-204.
Beijaard, F. (1992) *"And I promise you ...." Politics, economy and housing policy in Bolivia, 1952-1987*, Vrije Universiteit Amsterdam.
Bennett, V. (1989) 'Urban public services and social conflict: water in Monterrey', in Gilbert, A.G. (ed.)*Housing and land in urban Mexico*, Center of US-Mexican Studies, University of California, 79-100.
Berry, R.A. (1975) 'Open unemployment as a social problem in urban Colombia: myth and reality', *Economic Development and Cultural Change* 23, 276-91.
Birkbeck, C. (1979) 'Garbage, industry, and the "vultures" of Cali, Colombia', in Bromley, R. and Gerry, C. (eds.), 161-84.
Bogotá, Empresa del Agua y Acueducto de Bogotá (EAAB) (1968) Historia del agua en Bogotá, Bogotá.
Bonilla, F. (1970) 'Rio's favelas: the rural slum within the city', in Mangin, W. (ed.), 72-84.
Boran, A. (1989) 'Popular movements in Brazil: a case study of the movement for the defence of favelados in São Paulo', *Bulletin of Latin American Research* 8, 83-110.
Bortz, J. (1991) 'Problems and prospects in the Mexican and borderlands economies', *Mexican Studies* 7, 303-18.

Bromley, R. (1978) 'Organization, regulation and exploitation in the so-called 'urban informal sector': the street traders of Cali, Colombia', *World Development* 6, 1161-72.

Bromley, R. and Gerry, C. (eds.) (1979) *Casual work and poverty in Third World cities*, John Wiley & Sons.

Buchhofer, E. and Aguilar, A.G. (1991) 'La crisis reciente en la economía mexicana: respiro en el crecimiento de la Ciudad de México', *Revista Interamericana de Planificación 24, 176-207.*

Bunster, X. and Chaney, E. (1985) *Sellers and servants*, Praeger.

Burbach, R. and Flynn, P. (1980) *Agribusiness in the Americas*, Monthly Review Press.

Burgess, R. (1978) 'Petty commodity housing or dweller control? A critique of John Turner's view on housing policy', *World Development* 6, 1105-34.

Burgess, R. (1982) 'Self-help housing advocacy: a curious form of radicalism. A critique of the work of John F.C. Turner', in Ward (ed.) (1982), 56-98.

Burns, E. (1989) 'Squatters' power in San Miguel Teotongo', *NACLA Report on the Americas* 23, 29-35.

Butterworth, D (1962) 'A study of the urbanization among Mixtec migrants from Tilantongo in Mexico City', *América Indígena* 22, 257-74. Reproduced in Mangin, W. (ed.) (1970), Houghton Mifflin.

Butterworth, D. and Chance, J. (1981) *Latin American urbanization*, Cambridge University Press.

Cabrera, A. *et al.* (1986) *Los movimientos cívicos*, CINEP.

Câmara, A.P.R. (1991) Socio-spatial segregation and the level of public transportation in Rio de Janeiro, Brazil, Unpublished Ph.D. thesis, University College London.

Cardoso, F.H. (1975) 'The city and politics', in Hardoy, J.E. (ed.), 157-190.

Carroll, A. (1980) *Pirate subdivisions and the market for residental lots in Bogotá*, The City Study, World Bank.

Castells, M. (1977) *The urban question*, Edward Arnold.

Castells, M. (1983) *The city and the grassroots*, Edward Arnold.

CED (Centro de Estudios del Desarrollo) (1990) *Santiago: dos ciudades*, CED.

Chang, R. (1969) 'Historia del desarrollo telefónico en la ciudad de Caracas', in Tóvar, A. (ed.) *Estudio de Caracas, población y servicios urbanos*, Ediciones de la Biblioteca UCV, 327-350.

Chant, S. (1985) 'Single-parent families: choice or constraint? The formation of female-headed households in Mexican shanty towns', *Development and Change* 16, 635-56.

Chant, S. (1991) *Women and survival in Mexican cities: perspectives on gender, labour markets and low-income households*, Manchester University Press.

Chant, S. (1992) 'Migration at the margins: gender, poverty and population movement on the Costa Rican periphery', in Chant (ed.) *Gender and migration in developing countries*, Belhaven, 49-72.

Chant, S. (ed.) (1992) *Gender and migration in developing countries*, Belhaven.

Cifuentes, J.I. (c1979) Urban transportation in Bogotá, Paper prepared for the World Bank City Study.

Cleaves, P.S. (1974) *Bureaucratic politics and administration in Chile*, California University Press.

Cline, W.R. (1991) Facilitating labor adjustment in Latin America. Unpublished document prepared for Inter-American Development Bank, October 1991.

Collier, D. (1976) *Squatters and oligarchs*, John Hopkins University Press.

Collier, S., Blakemore, H. and Skidmore, T.E. (eds.)(1985) *The Cambridge Encyclopedia of Latin America and the Caribbean*, Cambridge University Press.

Collins, J.L. (1988) *Unseasonal migrations: the effects of rural labor scarcity in Peru*, Princeton University Press.

Connolly, P. (1990) 'Housing and the state in Mexico', in Shidlo, G. (ed.), 5-32.

Cordera Campos, R. and González Tiburcio, E. (1990) Crisis and transition in the Mexican economy, in González, M. and Escobar, A. (eds.) 19-56.

Cornelius, W. (1975) *Politics and the migrant poor in Mexico City*, Stanford University Press.

Cornelius, W. (1991) '*Los migrantes de la crisis*: the changing profile of Mexican migration to the United States', in González, M.and Escobar, A. (eds.), 155-94.

Coulomb, R. and Duhau, E. (eds.) (1988) *La ciudad y sus actores: conflictos y estrategias socioespaciales frente a las transformaciones de los centros urbanos*, Universidad Autónoma Metropolitana, Mexico City.

Coulomb, R. and Duhau, E. (eds.) (1989) *Políticas urbanas y urbanización de la política*, Universidad Autónoma Metropolitana, Mexico City.

Coulomb, R. and Sánchez, C. (1991) *¿Todos proprietarios? Vivienda de alquiler y sectores populares en la Ciudad de México*, CENVI, Mexico City.

Cubitt, T. (1988) *Latin American society*, Longman. ·

CVG (Corporación Venezolana de Guayana) (1987) *Estadísticas de la región Guayana, 1986*, Ciudad Guayana.

DANE (1991) *Censo económico nacional y multisectorial 1990*, Bogotá.

Davis, K. and Hertz, H. (1954) 'Urbanization and the development of pre-industrial areas', *Economic Development and Cultural Change* 4, 6-26.

Daykin, D.S. (1978) Urban planning and quality of life in Ciudad Guayana, Venezuela, unpublished doctoral dissertation, Vanderbilt University.

del Rio, V. (1992) 'Urban design and conflicting city images of Brazil', *Cities* 9, 270-79.

de Ramón, A. (1985) 'Vivienda', in de Ramón, A. and Gross, P. (eds.) *Santiago de Chile: características histórico ambientales, 1891-1924*, Monografías de Nueva Historia, Institute of Latin American Studies, 79-94.

de Soto, H. (1989) *The other path*, I.B. Tauris.

DESAL (ed.) (1969) *Marginalidad en América Latina*, Herder.

Dietz, H.A. (1987) 'Rent seeking, rent avoidance, and informality in analyses of Third World urban housing', paper delivered at Center of US-Mexican Studies, University of California, San Diego, 7-10 April 1987.

Dixon, W.J. (1987) 'Progress in the provision of basic human needs: Latin America, 1960-1980', *Journal of Developing Areas* 21, 129-40.

Doughty, P.L. (1970) 'Behind the back of the city: 'provincial' life in Lima, Peru', in Mangin, W. (ed.), 30-46.

Drake, P. (1989) 'Debt and democracy in Latin America, 1920s-1980s', in Stallings, B. and Kaufman, R. (eds.) *Debt and democracy in Latin America*, Westview Press, 39-58.

Dupuy, G. *et al.* (1987) *La crise des reseaux d'infrastructure: le cas de Buenos Aires*, Ecole Nationale des Ponts et Chaussées, Université Paris XII.

Durand, J. and Massey, D.S. (1992) 'Mexican migration to the United States: a critical view', *Latin American Research Review* 27, 3-42.

Eckstein, S. (1977) *The poverty of revolution*, Princeton University Press.

Eckstein, S. (ed.) (1989) *Power and popular protest: Latin American social movements*, University of California Press.

Eckstein, S. (1990a) 'Poor people versus the state and capital: anatomy of a successful community mobilization for housing in Mexico City', *International Journal of Urban and Regional Research*, 14, 274-96.

Eckstein, S. (1990b) 'Urbanization revisited: inner-city slum of hope and squatter settlement of despair', *World Development* 18, 165-82.

Economist, The (1990) *The Economist book of vital world statistics*, Hutchinson.

Economist, The (1993) *A survey of Mexico*, 13 February 1993.

Engels, F. (1872) *The housing question*, Progress Publishers, reprinted 1975.

Epstein, E. (1989) 'Austerity and trades unions in Latin America', in Canak, W.L. (ed.) *Lost promises: debt, austerity, and development in Latin America*, Westview Press, 169-89.

Evers, T. (1985) 'Identity: the hidden side of new social movements in Latin America', in Slater, D. (ed.) *New social movements and the state in Latin America*, Foris, 43-71.

Fernández-Kelly, P. (1983) *For we are sold, I and my people*, State University of New York Press.

Figueroa, O. (1990) 'La desregulación del transporte colectivo en Santiago: balances de diez años', *Revista EURE* 49, 23-32.

Figueroa, O. and Henry, E. (1988) 'Diagnóstico de los metros en América Latina', Revista EURE, 14, 42, 7-17.

Fresneda, O., Sarmiento, L., Muñoz, M. *et al.* (1991) *Pobreza, violencia y desigualdad: retos para la nueva Colombia*, Proyecto Regional para la Superación de la Pobreza, Programa de las Naciones Unidas para el Desarrollo, Bogotá.

Fuensalida, C. (1987) Informe sobre saneamiento de Santiago, Confederación mundial de ciudades metropolitanas, mimeo.

Fyfe, A. (1989) *Child labour*, Polity Press.

Garza, G. (1991) Dinámica industrial de la ciudad de México, 1940-1988, mimeo.

Garza, G. *et al.* (eds.) (1987) *Atlas de la ciudad de México*, Departamento del Distrito Federal y El Colegio de México.

Gay, R. (1990) 'Neighbourhood associations and political change in Rio de Janeiro', *Latin American Research Review* 25, 102-18.

Geertz, C. (1973) *Agricultural involution*, University of California Press.

Genatios, E. (1969) 'Historia de los acueductos de Caracas', in Továr, A. (ed.) *Estudio de Caracas, población y servicios urbanos*, Ediciones de la Biblioteca UCV, 259-326.

Germani, G. (1973) 'Urbanization, social change, and the great transformation', in Germani (ed.) *Modernization, urbanization and the urban crisis*, Little, Brown & Co., 3-58.

Gilbert A.G. (1974) *Latin American development: a geographical perspective*, Penguin

Gilbert, A.G. (1978) 'Bogotá: politics, planning and the crisis of lost opportunities', in Cornelius, W.A. and Kemper, R.V. (eds.) (1978) *Latin American Urban Research vol. 6*, Sage, 87-126.

Gilbert, A.G. (1989) 'Housing during recession: illustrations from Latin America', *Housing Studies* 4, 155-66.

Gilbert, A.G.(1990a) *Latin America*, Routledge.

Gilbert, A.G. (1990b) 'Urbanization at the periphery: reflections on the changing dynamics of housing and employment in Latin American cities', in Drakakis-Smith, D.W. (ed.) *Economic growth and urbanization in developing areas*, Routledge, 73-124.

Gilbert, A.G. and Varley, A. (1991)*Landlord and tenant: housing the poor in urban Mexico*, Routledge.

Gilbert, A.G. and Gugler, J. (1992a)*Cities, poverty and development: urbanization in the Third World*, Oxford University Press (second edition).

Gilbert, A.G. (1992b) 'Third World cities: Housing, infrastructure and services', *Urban Studies* 29, 435-60.

Gilbert, A.G. (1993) *In search of a home*, UCL Press.

Gilbert, A.G., Hardoy, J.E. and Ramírez, R. (eds.) (1982), *Urbanization in contemporary Latin America*, John Wiley.

Gilbert, A.G. and Ward, P.M. (1985) *Housing, the state and the poor: policy and practice in three Latin American cities*, Cambridge University Press.

Gilbert, A.G. and Ward, P. (1986) 'Latin American migrants: a tale of three cities' in Slater, F. (ed.) *Peoples and Environments: issues and enquiries*, Collins Educational, 24-42.

Gilbert, R. (1988) 'Rio de Janeiro', *Cities* 5, 2-9.

Glewwe, P. and Hall, G. (1992) Poverty and inequality during unorthodox adjustment: the case of Peru, 1985-90, Working Paper No. 86, The World Bank.

González de la Rocha, M. (1990) 'Family well-being, food consumption, and survival strategies during Mexico's economic crisis', in González, M. and Escobar, A. (eds.) *Social responses to Mexico's economic crisis of the 1980s*, University of California, 115-28.

González, M. and Escobar, A. (eds.)(1990) *Social responses to Mexico's economic crisis of the 1980s*. La Jolla: Centre for US-Mexican Studies, University of California,.

Goodman, D. and Redclift, M. (1981) *From peasant to proletarian: capitalist development and agrarian transition*, Blackwell.

Graham, C. (1992) 'The politics of protecting the poor during adjustment: Bolivia's Emergency Social Fund', *World Development* 20, 1233-51.

Green, D. (1992) *Faces of Latin America,* Latin America Bureau.

Grindle, M.S. (1988) *Searching for rural development: labor migration and employment in Mexico,* Cornell University Press.

Gwynne, R.N. (1990) *New horizons? Third world industrialization in an international framework,* Longman.

Haber, P.L. (1990) Cárdenas, Salinas and urban popular movements in Mexico: the case of el Comité de Defensa Popular, General Franciso Villa de Durango, Institute of Latin American Studies, mimeo.

Hahner, J.E. (1986) *Poverty and politics: the urban poor in Brazil, 1870-1920,* University of New Mexico Press.

Hakkert, R. and Goza, F.W. (1989) 'The demographic consequences of austerity in Latin America', in Canak, W.L. (ed.) *Lost promises: debt, austerity, and development in Latin America,* Westview Press, 69-97.

Hardoy, J.E. (1975) 'Two thousand years of Latin American urbanization', in Hardoy (ed.), 3-56.

Hardoy, J.E. (ed.) (1975) *Urbanization in Latin America: approaches and issues,* Anchor Books.

Hardoy, J.E., Mitlin, D. and Satterthwaite, D. (1992) *Environmental problems in third world cities,* Earthscan.

Harris, N. (1987) *The end of the third world,* Penguin.

Harris, N. (ed.) (1992) *Cities in the 1990s: the challenge for developing countries,* UCL Press.

Hellinger, D.C. (1991) *Venezuela: tarnished democracy,* Westview Press.

Herzog, L.A. (1990) *Where north meets south: cities, space and politics on the United States-Mexican border,* Centre for Mexican American Studies, University of Texas.

Hirata, H. and Humphrey, J. (1991) 'Workers' responses to job loss: female and male industrial workers in Brazil', *World Development* 19, 671-82.

Hoselitz, B.F. (1957) 'Generative and parasitic cities', *Economic Development and Cultural Change* 3, 278-94.

Humphrey, J. (1992) Are the unemployed part of the urban poverty problem? Institute of Development Studies at the University of Sussex, mimeo.

Iglesias, E.V. (1992) *Reflections on economic development: toward a new Latin American consensus,* Inter-American Development Bank.

India, NIUA (National Institute of Urban Affairs) (1989) *Rental housing in India: an overview, NIUA Research Study Series no. 31.*

INE (Instituto Nacional de Estadística) (1986) *Perú: compendio estadístico, 1985,* Lima.

INEGI (Instituto Nacional de Estadística, Geografía e Informática) (1989)*Encuesta nacional de empleo urbano: indicadores trimestrales de empleo Cd. de Guadalajara (oct-dic de 1988).*

Inter-American Development Bank, (1992) Report on the eighth general increase in the resources of the Inter-American Development Bank, mimeo.

Janssen, R. (1978) 'Class practices of dwellers in *barrios populares*, the struggle for the right to the city', *International Journal of Urban and Regional Research* 2, 147-59.

Jongkind, C.F. (1974) 'A reappraisal of the role of regional associations in Lima, Peru', *Comparative Studies in Society and History* 16, 471-82.

Klak, T. (1990) 'Spatially and socially progressive state policy and programs: the case of Brazil's National Housing Bank', *Annals of the Association of American Geographers* 80, 571-89.

Kowarick, L. and Bonduki, N. (1988) 'Espaço urbano e espaço político: do populismo à redemocratização', in Kowarick, L. (ed.), 133-168.

Kowarick, L. and Ant, C. (1988) 'Cem anos de promiscuidade: o cortiço na cidade de São Paulo', in Kowarick, L. (ed.), 49-74.

Kowarick, L. (ed.) (1988) *As lutas sociais e a cidade: São Paulo: passado e presente*, Paz e Terra.

Kowarick, L. (1991) 'Ciudad & ciudadanía. Metrópolis del subdesarrollo industrializado', *Nueva Sociedad* 114, 84-93.

Kusnetzoff, F. (1975) 'Housing policies or housing politics: an evaluation of the Chilean experience', *Journal of Interamerican Studies and World Affairs* 7, 281-309.

Kusnetzoff, F. (1990) 'The state and housing in Chile - regime types and policy choices', in Shidlo, G. (ed.), 48-66.

Laite, J. (1984) 'Migration and social differentiation amongst Mantaro valley peasants', in Long, N. and Roberts, B., 107-39.

Lautier, B. (1990) 'Wage relationship, formal sector and employment policy in South America', *Journal of Development Studies* 26, 278-98.

Lawson, V.A. (1992) 'Industrial subcontracting and employment forms in Latin America: a framework for contextual analysis', *Progress in Human Geography* 16, 1-23.

Lerner, D. (1967) 'Comparative analysis of processes of modernization', in Miner, H. (ed.) *The city in modern Africa*, Pall Mall, 21-38.

Lewis, O. (1959) *Five families: Mexican case studies in the culture of poverty*, Basic Books.

Lewis, O. (1966) 'The culture of poverty', *Scientific American* 215, 19-25.

Linn, J.F. (1983) *Cities in the developing world: policies for their equitable and efficient growth*, Oxford University Press.

Lizt Mendoza, S. (1988) 'Repuestas del transporte urbano en las zonas marginadas', in Benítez, R and Benigno Morelos, J. (eds.) *Grandes problemas de la ciudad de México*, Plaza y Valdés, 215-42.

Lloyd, P. (1981) *The young towns of Lima*, Cambridge University Press.

Long, N. and Roberts, B. (1984) *Miners, peasants and entrepreneurs: regional development in the Central Highlands of Peru*, Cambridge University Press.

Mainwaring, S. (1989) 'Grassroots popular movements and the struggle for democracy: Nova Iguaçu', in Stepan, A. (ed.) *Democratizing Brazil: problems of transition and consolidation*, Oxford University Press, 168-204.

Mangin, W. (1967)'Latin American squatter settlements: a problem and a solution', *Latin American Research Review* 2, 65-98.

Mangin , W. (ed.) (1970) *Peasants in cities: readings in the anthropology of urbanization*, Houghton Mifflin.

Mangin, W. (1970a) 'Urbanization case history in Peru', in Mangin , W. (ed.) , 47-54.

Mangin, W. (1970b) 'Tales from the barriadas', in Mangin, W. (ed.), 55-61.

Mathey, K. (ed.) (1992) *Beyond self-help housing*, Profil Verlag and Mansell Publishing.

Matos Mar, J. (1968) *Urbanización y barriadas en América del Sur*, Instituto de Estudios Peruanos.

Mazumdar, D. (1989) Microeconomic issues of labor markets in developing countries, *EDI Seminar Paper no. 40*, World Bank.

McGee, T.G. (1976) 'The persistence of the proto-proletariat: occupational structures and planning for the future of Third World cities', *Progress in Geography* 9, 3-38.

Meller, P. (1991) 'Adjustment and social costs in Chile during the 1980s', *World Development* 19, 1545-61.

Merrick, T.W. (1986) 'Population pressures in Latin America', *Population Bulletin* 41, number 3.

Mohan, R. and Hartline, N. (1984) The poor of Bogotá; who they are, what they do, and where they live, *World Bank Staff Working Papers No. 635*.

Moises, J.A. and Stolkce, V. (1987) 'Urban transport and popular violence in Brazil', in Archetti, E.P. et al. (eds.) *Sociology of Developing Societies: Latin America*, 229-40.

Molinero, A. (1991) 'Mexico City Metropolitan Area case study', *Built Environment* 17, 122-37.

Morales, S. (1988) 'El metro de Santiago', *Revista EURE* 42, 19-41.

Morfín, G.A. and Sánchez, M. (1984) 'Controles jurídicos y psicosociales en la producción de espacio urbano para sectores populares en Guadalajara',*Encuentro* 1, 115-41.

Morris, A. (1978) 'Urban growth patterns in Latin America with illustrations from Caracas', *Urban Studies* 15, 299-312.

Morse, R. (1958) *From community to metropolis: a biography of São Paulo*, Yale University Press.

Morse, R. (1965) 'Recent research on Latin American urbanization: a selective survey with commentary', *Latin American Research Review* 1, 35-74.

Myers, D. (1978) 'Caracas: the politics of intensifying primacy', in Cornelius, W. and Kemper, R.V. (eds.) *Latin American Urban Research* 6, 227-58.

Necochea, A. (1987) 'El allegamiento de los sin tierra, estrategia de supervivencia en vivienda',*Revista Latinoamericana de Estudios Urbanos-Regionales (EURE)* 13-14, 85-100.

Newson, L. (1987) 'The Latin American colonial experience', in Preston, D. (ed.) *Latin American development: geographical perspectives*, Longman, 7-33.

OCEI (Oficina Central de Estadística e Informática) (1985) *XI censo general de población y vivienda*, Caracas.

Ogrodnik, E. (1984) 'Encuesta a los allegados en el Gran Santiago', *Revista de Economía* 22.

Oliveira, O. de and García, B. (1990) 'Recesión económica y cambio en los determinantes del trabajo femenino', mimeo. El Colegio de México.

Oliveira, O de, (1991) 'Migration of women, family organization and labour markets in Mexico', in Jelín, E. (ed.) *Family, household and gender relations in Latin America*, Routledge and UNESCO, 101-18.

Oliveira, F. de (1985) 'A critique of dualist reason: the Brazilian economy since 1930', in Bromley, R. (ed.) *Planning for small enterprises in Third World cities*, Pergamon, 65-95. (First published in Portuguese in 1972.)

Ovalles, O. and Córdoba, K. (1986) 'La calidad de vida en el área metropolitana de Caracas, Venezuela', in Ibarra, V. et al. (eds.) *La ciudad y el medio ambiente en América Latina*, El Colegio de México, 61-96.

Oxhorn, P. (1991) 'The popular sector response to an authoritarian regime: shantytown organizations since the military coup', *Latin American Perspectives* 18, 66-91.

Palmer, D.C. (ed.) (1992) *The shining path of Peru: a study of Sendero Luminoso*, Hurst and Co.

Pearce, J. (1990) *Colombia: inside the labyrinth*, Latin America Bureau.

Peattie, L. (1987) 'An idea in good currency and how it grew: the informal sector', *World Development* 15, 851-60.

Peek, P. and Standing, G. (eds.) (1982) *State policies and migration*, Croom Helm.

Peil, M. and Sada, P.O. (1984) *African urban society*, John Wiley.

Perlman, Janice (1976) *The myth of marginality*, University of California Press.

Perló-Cohen, M. (1981) *Estado, vivienda y estructura urbana en el Cardenismo: el caso de la Ciudad de México, Instituto de Investigaciones Sociales*, Universidad Nacional Autónoma de México.

Perna, C. (1981) *Evolución de la geografía urbana de Caracas*, Ediciones de la Facultad de Humanidades y Educación.

Pfeffermann, G.P. and Griffin, C.C. (1989) *Nutrition and health programs in Latin America: targeting social expenditures*, World Bank.

Philip, G. (ed.) (1988) *The Mexican economy*, Routledge.

Portes, A. (1972) 'Rationality in the slum: an essay in interpretive sociology', *Comparative Studies in Society and History* 14, 268-86.

Portes, A. (1979) 'Housing policy, urban poverty, and the state: the favelas of Rio de Janeiro, 1972-76', *Latin American Research Review* 14, 3-24.

Portes, A. (1990) 'Latin American urbanization during the years of the crisis', *Latin American Research Review* 25, 7-44.

Portes, A. and Benton, L. (1984) 'Industrial development and labor absorption: a reinterpretation', *Population and Development Review* 10, 589-611.

Portes, A. and Johns, M. (1986) 'Class structure and spatial polarization: an assessment of urban trends in the Third World', *Tijdschrift voor Economische en Sociale Geografie* 77, 378-88.

Pozas-Garza, M. (1989) 'Land settlement by the urban poor in Monterrey', in Gilbert, A.G. (ed.) *Housing and land in urban Mexico*, Center of US-Mexican Studies, University of California, 65-78.

Pradilla, E. (1978) 'Notas acerca del "problema de la vivienda"', *Ideología y Sociedad* 16, 70-107.

PREALC (International Labour Organisation's Regional Employment Programme in Latin America) (1984) 'El mercado del trabajo en la actual coyuntura', *Notas sobre la economía y el desarrollo* 403.

Quijano, A. (1974) 'The marginal pole of the economy and the marginalised labour force', *Economy and Society* 3, 393-428.

Radcliffe, S.A. (1990) 'Ethnicity, patriarchy, and incorporation into the nation: female migrants as domestic servants in Peru', *Environment and Planning D: Society and Space* 8, 379-93.

Radcliffe, S.A. (1992) 'Mountains, maidens and migration: gender, poverty and population movement on the Costa Rican periphery', in Chant, S. (ed.), 30-48.

Ray, T. (1969) *The politics of the barrios of Caracas*, University of California Press.

Revéiz, E. *et al.* (1977) *Poder e información*, Universidad de los Andes, Centro de Estudios sobre Desarrollo Económico.

Riofrío, G. (1978) *Se busca terreno para próxima barriada: espacios disponibles en Lima 1940, 1978, 1990*, DESCO.

Riofrío, G. (1991) 'Lima en los 90. Un acercamiento a la nueva dinámica urbana', *Nueva Sociedad* 114, 143-49.

Roberts, B. (1978) *Cities of peasants*, Edward Arnold.

Rodríguez, A. (1989) 'Santiago, viejos y nuevos temas', in Carrión, F. (ed.) *La investigación urbana en América Latina: caminos recorridos y por recorrer - Estudios nationales*, Ciudad, Quito, 203-36.

Roxborough, I. (1989) 'Organized labor: a major victim of the debt crisis', in Stallings, B. and Kaufman, R. (eds.) *Debt and democracy in Latin America*, Westview Press, 91-108.

Sachs, C. (1990) *São Paulo: politiques publiques et habitat populaire*, Editions de la Maison des Sciences de l'Homme.

Salmen, L.F. (1987) *Listen to the people*, Oxford University Press.

Sánchez-Albornoz, N. (1974) *The population of Latin America: a history*, University of California Press.

Sanderson, S.S. (ed.) (1985) *The Americas in the New International Division of Labor*, Holmes and Meier.

Santana, P. (1983) *Desarrollo regional y paros cívicos en Colombia*, CINEP.

Santana, P. (1989) *Los movimientos sociales en Colombia*. Ediciones Foro Nacional por Colombia.

Sargent, C.S. (1993) 'The Latin American city' in Blouet, B. and Blouet, O. (eds.) *Latin America and the Caribbean: a systematic and regional survey*, John Wiley, 172-216.

Sayer, C. (1991) 'The rise of Superbarrio', *Geographical Magazine,* February 23-4.
Scarpaci, J.L., Pio-Infante, R. and Gaete, A. (1988) 'Planning residential segregation: the case of Santiago, Chile', *Urban Geography* 9, 19-36.
Schneider, C. (1991) 'Mobilization at the grassroots: shantytowns and resistance in authoritarian Chile', *Latin American Perspectives* 18, 92-112.
Schuurmann, F. and van Naerssen, T. (eds.) (1989) *Urban social movements in the Third World,* Routledge.
Scobie, J. (1974) *Buenos Aires: plaza to suburb 1870-1910,* Oxford University Press.
Selby, H.A., Murphy, A.D. and Lorenzen, S.A. (1990) *The Mexican urban household: organizing for self-defense,* University of Texas Press.
Shaiken, H. (1990) *Mexico in the global economy: high technology and work organization in export industries,* Center for US-Mexican Studies, University of California.
Shidlo, G. (ed.) (1990) *Housing policy in developing countries,* Routledge.
Silva, A. (1992)*Imaginarios urbanos - Bogotá y São Paulo: cultura y comunicación urbana en América Latina,* Tercer Mundo.
Singer, P. (1982) 'Neighbourhood movements in São Paulo', in Safa, H.I. (ed.) *Towards a political economy of urbanization in Third World countries,*
Skeldon, R. (1990) *Population mobility in developing countries,* Belhaven Press.
Sklair, L. (1989) *Assembling for development,* Unwin Hyman.
Slater, D. (ed.) (1985) *New social movements and the state in Latin America,* Foris.
South, R.B. (1990) 'Transnational "maquiladora" location', *Annals of the American Association of American Geographers* 80, 549-70.
Standing, G. (1989) 'Global feminization through flexible labor', *World Development* 17, 1077-1096.
Stann, J. (1975) 'Transportation and urbanization in Caracas, 1891-1936', *Journal of Interamerican Studies and World Affairs* 17, 82-100.
Strong, S. (1992) *Shining path: the world's deadliest revolutionary force,* Harper Collins.
Suárez, H. (ed), Vivir en Bogotá, Ediciones Foro Nacional.

Tello, C. (1990) 'Combating poverty in Mexico', in González, M. and Escobar, A. (eds.) 19-56.
Tenjo, J. (1990) 'Opportunities, aspirations, and urban unemployment of youth: the case of Colombia', *Economic Development and Cultural Change* 38, 733-62.
Tipple, A.G. and Willis, K.G. (1991) 'Tenure choice in a West African city', *Third World Planning Review* 13, 27-46.
Tokman, V.E. (1978) 'Competition between the informal and formal sectors in retailing: the case of Santiago', *World Development,* 6, 1187-1198.
Tokman, V. (1989) 'Policies for a heterogeneous informal sector in Latin America', *World Development* 17, 1067-76.
Tolosa, H. (1992), Urban expansion and structural change in the Rio de Janeiro Metropolitan Area, mimeo.
Townsend, J. (1987) 'Rural change: progress for whom?', in Preston, D. (ed.)*Latin American development: geographical perspectives,* Longman, 199-228.

Turner, J.F.C. (1967) 'Barriers and channels for housing development in modernizing *countries'*, *Journal of the American Institute of Planners* 33, 167-81.

Turner, J.F.C. (1968) 'The squatter settlement: an architecture that works', *Architectural Design* 38, 357-60.

Turner, J.F.C. (1976) *Housing by people: towards autonomy in building environment*, Marion Boyars.

Turner, J.F.C. (1982) 'Issues in self-help and self-managed housing', in Ward (1982), 99-114.

United Nations (1987) *United Nations Statistical Yearbook 1987*, New York.

United Nations (1989) *1989 report on the world social situation*, New York.

United Nations, Department of International Economic and Social Affairs (1991) *World urbanization prospects 1990*, New York.

UNECLA (1973) 'Some consequences of urbanization for the total social structure', in Germani, G. (ed.) *Modernization, urbanization and the urban crisis*, Little, Brown & Co., 151-67.

UNECLAC (United Nations Commission for Latin America and the Caribbean)(1987) *Statistical yearbook for Latin America and the Caribbean 1987 edition*, New York.

UNECLAC (1990) *Magnitud de la pobreza en América Latina en los años 80*, Santiago.

UNECLAC (1991) *Statistical yearbook for Latin America and the Caribbean 1991 edition*, New York.

UNECLAC (1992) 'Preliminary overview of the Latin American and Caribbean Economy 1992', *Notas sobre la economía y el desarrollo*, 537/538.

Valladares, L. (1988) 'Urban sociology in Brazil: a research report', *International Journal of Urban and Regional Research* 12, 285-303.

Valladares, L. (1990) 'Family and child work in the favela', in Datta, S. (ed.) *Third World urbanization: reappraisals and new perspectives*, Swedish Council for Research in the Humanities and Social Sciences, 149-67.

van Garderen, T. (1989) in Schuurman, F. and van Naerssen, T. (eds.) *Urban social movements in the Third World*, Routledge, 27-44.

van Lindert, P. (1991) 'Moving up or staying down? Migrant-native differential mobility in La Paz', *Urban Studies* 28, 433-63.

Vargas, J. and Zambrano, F. (1988) 'Santa Fe y Bogotá: evolución histórica y servicios públicos (1600-1957)', in Santana, P. *et al. Bogotá 450 años; retos y realidades*, Foro Nacional por Colombia and Instituto Francés de Estudios Andinos, 11-92.

Vázquez, D. (1989) *Guadalajara: ensayos de interpretación*, El Colegio de Jalisco.

Villa, M. (1987) 'La politicización innecesaria: el régimen político mexicano y sus exigencias de pasividad ciudadana a los damnificados', *Estudios Demográficos y Urbanos* 4, 27-52.

Violich, F. (1944) *Cities of Latin America*, Reinhardt, Holt and Winston.

Violich, F. and Daughters, R. (1987) *Urban planning for Latin America: the challenge of metropolitan growth*, Oelgeschlager, Gunn and Hain.

Walker, G.P. (1991) Industrial disasters, vulnerability and planning in Third World cities, Paper presented at Staffordshire Polytechnic, September 1991.

Walton (1978) 'Guadalajara: creating the divided city', in Cornelius, W. and Kemper, R.V. (eds.) (1978) *Latin American Urban Research vol. 6.*, Sage, 25-50.

Walton, J. (1989) 'Debt, protest, and the state in Latin America', in Eckstein (ed.) 299-328.

Ward, B. (1964) 'The uses of prosperity', *Saturday Review*, 29 August 1964. Cited in Perlman (1976).

Ward, P.M. (1976) 'The squatter settlement as slum or housing solution: evidence from Mexico City', *Land Economics* 52, 330-346.

Ward, P.M. (ed.) (1982) *Self-help housing: a critique*, Mansell.

Ward, P.M. (1990) *Mexico City*, Belhaven.

Wario, E. (1984) 'Crecimiento urbano y acumulación de capital en el sector inmobiliario en el área urbana de Guadalajara', *Encuentro* 2, 146-66.

Webb, R. and Fernández, G. (1991) *Perú en números 1991*, Cuánto S.A.

Wilkie, J. and Perkal, A. (1984) *Statistical abstract for Latin America 23*, University of California, Los Angeles.

Wilkie, J., Lorey, D.E. and Ochoa, E. (1988) *Statistical abstract for Latin America 26*, University of California, Los Angeles.

Wilkie, J., Ochoa, E. and Lorey, D.E. (1990) *Statistical abstract for Latin America 28*, University of California, Los Angeles.

Winnie, W.W. (1987) *La encuesta de hogares de Guadalajara, 1986*, Universidad de Guadalajara.

World Bank (1991) *Urban policy and economic development: an agenda for the 1990s*, Washington D.C.

World Bank (1992a) *World development report 1992*, Washington D.C.

World Bank (1992b) *Governance and development*, Washington D.C.

World Bank (1992c) *Poverty reduction handbook*, Washington D.C.

World Bank (1993) *Housing: enabling markets to work*, Washington D.C.

Zatz, J. (1991) 'Energie dans les villes: le cas de São Paulo', *Cahiers du Brésil Contemporain* 16, 41-64.

INDEX

Books from the Latin America Bureau

ON THE LINE
Life on the US-Mexican Border
Augusta Dwyer

The border between Mexico and the US is a unique meeting point of the first and third worlds. For decades it has been a source of tension between Washington and Mexico City, as millions of impoverished Mexicans defy the US Border Patrol and head for the promised lands of California and other Southern States.

Now it has also become the prototype for the new relationship between the two countries, enshrined in the North American Free Trade Agreement (NAFTA). NAFTA will provide US industry with a vast pool of cheap labour, lax environmental regulations and an effective one-party state dedicated to keeping union protest to a minimum.

For 30 years a more restricted version of NAFTA has allowed US industries to set up cheap labour plants along the border. The 2,000 maquiladora factories are Mexico's fastest growing industrial sector, providing nearly 500,000 low wage jobs, most of them for young women.

In **On The Line**, Augusta Dwyer journeys along the length of the border, uncovering the stories of dozens of ordinary Mexicans - maquila workers, illegal migrants and environmental activists. She reveals the costs of free trade, and what Mexicans are doing to try to end their exploitation and the destruction of their environment.

1994 200 pages ISBN 0 906156 84 X (pbk) £10.00

THE LATIN AMERICAN LEFT
From the Fall of Allende to Perestroika
Barry Carr & Steve Ellner (eds)

With the collapse of the eastern bloc and the rise of neo-liberalism, the Left appears increasingly isolated in many parts of the world. In Latin America, however, despite Cuba's economic crisis and the disintegration of orthodox communism, the Left has emerged from decades of dictatorship and repression with new identities and forms of participation.

In eight country studies, contributors examine the failure of the 1960s guerrilla strategies, the challenge posed by the new social movements and the new emphasis on democratic reforms over socioeconomic change. Looking at the erosion of US influence in Latin America and the social impact of structural adjustment policies, the book also explores regional issues such as trade union struggles and guerrilla warfare.

1993 256 pages   ISBN 0 906156 72 6 (pbk) £14.00

Published in North America by Westview Press

OUT OF THE SHADOWS
Women, Resistance and Politics in South America
Jo Fisher

In **Out of the Shadows**, author Jo Fisher interviews women in Argentina, Chile, Uruguay and Paraguay to show how they moved into the vacuum left by the military's destruction of the male-dominated left. Chapters describe how women have organised - in communal kitchens in Chile's shantytowns, as trade unionists in Uruguay, peace activists in Paraguay, mothers of the disappeared and self-help groups in Argentina, as grassroots feminists in Chile - ending the isolation of home life.

While built around the traditional female concerns such as providing food and care for their families, the new women's movements have developed a grassroots feminism that is strikingly different from the middle class feminism of the city centres and have had a seismic impact on gender consciousness throughout the region.

" A fascinating and vivid insight into the rise of the independent women's movement in South America." Maxine Molyneux, University of London

"Read it and encounter hope renewed." *Everywoman*

1993 200 pages ISBN 0 906156 77 7 (pbk) £9.00/$19.00

PERU: TIME OF FEAR
Deborah Poole and Gerardo Rénique

Since 1980 Peru has been the scene of an escalating civil war. On the one hand, the Sendero Luminoso ('Shining Path') Maoists determined to destroy existing society. On the other, the Peruvian military, acknowledged as South America's worst human rights violators.

Caught in the middle, and dying in their thousands each year, are the poor peasants and slum-dwellers of Peru. Victims also of a collapsing economy and radical austerity programme, the great majority of Peruvians are living a time of fear.

"Deborah Poole and Gerardo Rénique have managed to write a concise, accessible, lucid and fair-minded book on 20th-century Peruvian politics that leaves earlier efforts in the shade." *Village Voice*

"...another authoritative country profile...compelling and convincing." *New Internationalist*

1992 220 pages ISBN 0 906156 70 X (pbk) £9.00 /$19.00

Prices are for paperback editions and include postage and packing.

LAB books are available by post from Latin America Bureau, 1 Amwell Street, London EC1R 1UL. Cheques payable to LAB. Write for a free catalogue.

US$ orders for LAB books should be sent to Monthly Review Press, 122 West 27th Street, New York, NY 10001. Cheques payable to Monthly Review Press.